D0207947

Takings Law
and the Supreme Court

Studies in Law and Politics

David A. Schultz
General Editor

Vol. 3

PETER LANG
New York • Washington, D.C./Baltimore • Boston
Bern • Frankfurt am Main • Berlin • Vienna • Paris

George Skouras

Takings Law
and the Supreme Court

Judicial Oversight
of the Regulatory State's
Acquisition, Use, and Control
of Private Property

PETER LANG
New York • Washington, D.C./Baltimore • Boston
Bern • Frankfurt am Main • Berlin • Vienna • Paris

Library of Congress Cataloging-in-Publication Data

Skouras, George.
Takings law and the Supreme Court: judicial oversight of the regulatory state's
acquisition, use, and control of private property / George Skouras.
p. cm. — (Studies in law and politics; 3)
Includes bibliographical references and index.
1. Land use—Law and legislation—United States. 2. Eminent domain—
United States. 3. Right of property—United States. 4. Judicial review—
United States. I. Title. II. Series: Studies in law
and politics (New York, N.Y.); vol. 3.
KF5698.S58   346.7304'5—dc21   97-5195
ISBN 0-8204-3816-2
ISSN 1083–3366

Die Deutsche Bibliothek-CIP-Einheitsaufnahme

Skouras, George:
Takings law and the supreme court: judicial oversight of the regulatory state's
acquisition, use, and control of private property / George Skouras. –New York;
Washington, D.C./Baltimore; Boston; Bern; Frankfurt am Main; Berlin;
Vienna; Paris: Lang.
(Studies in law and politics; 3)
ISBN 0-8204-3816-2

The paper in this book meets the guidelines for permanence and durability
of the Committee on Production Guidelines for Book Longevity
of the Council of Library Resources.

Printed in the United States of America.

For my family,
Dora Skouras, John Skouras, and Angela Skouras

ACKNOWLEDGMENTS

It is a pleasure to acknowledge the many people that have been of help to me over the years in completing this book. I want to thank each and everyone of them.

Professor Jacob Landynski, New School for Social Research, Graduate Faculty of Political & Social Science, has for many years provided me advise and commentary on my work. I am grateful to Professor Victoria Hattam, Graduate Faculty, for her advise and comments on earlier drafts of this work. Professor David Schultz, University of Minnesota and series editor, has made important suggestions for the improvement of this book. David Schultz provided me with commentary that has been helpful in the examination and analysis of many sections of this work.

I want to thank Reynolds Russell for his assistance in editing an earlier draft of this work and his useful comments. Patricia Olney, Ph.D. Candidate in political science at the University of Miami, has provided me with a close analytical reading of part two of this work. I am grateful to Owen Lancer, the Acquisitions Editor at Peter Lang Publishing, Lisa Dillon, Production Supervisor, Sara Gillespie, Productions Assistant, and the rest of the production team.

I was fortunate many years ago, as a third year law student at Rutgers Law School, to be introduced to the subject of takings jurisprudence by Professor Vicki Been.

I also want to thank the following institutions for use of their facilities: New York University, Cardozo Law School, and the Graduate Faculty.

But most of all, I want to thank my family, Dora, John, and Angela. This book would not have been possible without them.

The views and positions taken here do not necessarily reflect those of the named above, and I am solely responsible for all remaining errors.

TABLE OF CONTENTS

Part II

THEORIES OF TAKINGS LAW AND PROPERTY
(1) MIDDLE RANGE THEORY: LEGAL, ECONOMIC, AND POLITICAL
(2) ADVANCED THEORY: PHILOSOPHY OF PROPERTY AND TAKINGS LAW

INTRODUCTION

The current state of regulatory takings law, as applied to land use, is a patchwork of fixes that make generalization a hazardous exercise. In an era of deregulation and dismantling of the New Deal state apparatus, this work takes the position that a weak federal state is a bad idea. The current land use system is more akin to a system of fiefdoms than to anything else. The Supreme Court has resorted to its own devices to resolve land use problems. This work will show that the Supreme Court has been unable to develop a cohesive land use policy without Federal governmental participation. The results have been land use policy through *ad hoc* Court rulings.

Currently, property rights groups are out front pushing for deregulation of property interests. They are pushing for a strictly nineteenth century version of the common law. The emergence of new militia groups has stirred up Congress. Frustrated property owners believe they are over-taxed and over-regulated. This work will argue that the problem is not one of over-regulation or under-regulation but one of rational regulation.

Property rights groups make the assumption that the culprit for much of the over-regulation is the New Deal. In part this is correct, but this is only half of the story. What these groups overlook is that the Framers of the Constitution created a compound republic rather than a unitary state. The structure of a compound republic is more susceptible to the inefficient use of public resources than is a unitary state, but not necessarily so. Madisonian checks and balances are costly devices.

This work claims that changes in social, demographic, geographic, and technological structure has undermined the nineteenth century version of common law solutions to property problems. And the Supreme Court has not been able to resolve land use problems satisfactorily because of the lack of Federal leadership on these issues. The Supreme Court does not have the resources to adequately deal with land use as shown by its *ad hoc* methodology of dealings with regulatory takings issues. The result has been a feudal network of waste, inefficiency, and unfair legal outcomes.

This work assumes that the administrative state is not antithetical to democratic principles. Bureaucracies have their positive as well as negative aspects. Bureaucracies, not disciplined by markets, can become inefficient, bloated, and wasteful of public resources, but markets are not the only means of disciplining large agencies. There is no inherent reason why bureaucracies could not become efficient if there is a correct mix or rewards and punishments. Behavior modification can be used to discipline bureaucratic behavior. But efficiency is not the only consideration. Agencies need not only be efficient but fair. The criteria for "fairness" is not as simple as counting dollars.

More specifically this work will cover "takings" law based on the Fifth Amendment to the United States Constitution—"nor shall private property be taken for public use without just compensation" and as made applicable to the States through the Fourteenth Amendment. The aim of this work is to study the development of Federal takings jurisprudence since the 1870's. The development of case law will set the pace of the first part, and its theoretical analysis will set the pace of the second part. Some of the theorists were selected because their work has achieved classic status in the field. The others were selected in order to present a broad range of approaches to the takings field.

The tension between the takings clause and police power regulations will be explored. This tension has been exacerbated due to the entanglement of the police power with the takings power in 1922 with the case of *Pennsylvania Coal Co. v. Mahon*. This new category of regulatory takings will prove to be controversial and problematic.

The general thesis of this work is that the Supreme Court has failed to provide lower courts with the guidance necessary to adequately deal with regulatory takings problems. The balancing tests that the Court uses to determine a taking lack a solid foundation and are rather malleable creatures. Consequently, the field of land use law has been unstable, unpredictable, and muddled. More recently, the Supreme Court has been swinging between balancing tests and formal rules in recognition of the instability of its rulings on takings issues. If the problem with balancing tests is malleability, the problem with formal rules is inflexibility. That is, due to the continuous criticism of the Supreme Court's balancing tests, the Court in recent years has tilted toward formalism, developing *per se* rules to deal with regulatory takings rather than simply relying on balancing the various interests. The concept of formalism will be treated in the theoretical part of this study.

It will be argued that the Court's recent push for a nineteenth century common law approach to late twentieth century land use problems is wrong. This work will argue that the nineteenth century political and legal framework is not adequate to deal with modern problems of land use. It will further be argued that emphasis on localism is inadequate to deal with land use issues that cross state and national borders. Global interdependence has undermined the traditional notion that land use is of a local concern. It will be shown that the Supreme Court has had a discontinuous role in the field and uneven grasp of land use law. This has led to a series of land use opinions that contribute to inefficiency, unproductivness, and waste. And, consequently, these legal determinations have not served the American people well.

The proposed solution is for local land use policies be more closely supervised at the State and Federal level, if there is to be a more efficient utilization of land and greater protection for ecologically sensitive areas and threats to the environment. The piecemeal and patchwork approach to takings law has confused regulatory agencies. Although this work focuses on the Supreme Court's attempts to deal with regulatory takings, the Court should not be singled out for special criticism when the Federal government has only indirectly and haphazardly dealt with land use problems at the local level.

Today, it is taken for granted that the Supreme Court no longer provides the level of judicial review for property/economic matters that it provides for civil rights concerns. Nor does it provide counterweight to the legislative process, in property/economic concerns, that it once did. Since the late 1930's, it is commonly believed that the Supreme Court has pulled up stakes in reviewing property/economic legislation. Basically, what the legislature wants, it gets, with the Court passively providing minimal judicial review. Although this view is correct for the most part, it does underestimate the Court's role as the final interpreter of the Constitution. And the Court has not exactly pulled up stakes altogether. The Court still possesses considerable power in the field of land use and is prepared to use it to *modify* the state's legislative agenda through its interpretation of the Fifth and Fourteenth Amendments, but its lack of direction has led to a confusing set of legal statements and a jumbled set of tests in handling takings cases.

With the rise of the regulatory state during President Franklin Delano Roosevelt's New Deal, the common law has been hampered and battered by regulatory approaches to social problems. Although the Court was attacked in the 1930's for upholding traditional common law solutions to property interference, it slowly managed to recover to the point where the common law is no longer seen as a relic of a bygone era. Whether the common law can continue to serve as a potent force in modern civil society is a questionable proposition. Regulatory tools should be given an opportunity to assist, and replace if need be, common law solutions to social problems. This work does not advocate that the common law tradition be overturned—only that it be tolerant of innovative regulatory ideas, when it no longer can meet modern social needs. The current trend is to cut down Federal agencies and return to more common law solutions for social and economic problems.

Although the takings clause was overshadowed in the early part of the twentieth century by the substantive due process and liberty of contract doctrines, as the principal means of protecting private property, the takings clause has emerged as the principal doctrinal means to protect private property since the demise of the other two doctrines.

As of today, the regulatory state has not been able to displace the common law. It will be seen that although zoning is a powerful regulatory tool, it has not been able to displace the common law tradition of dealing with land use nuisance problems. And, currently, under the influence of the Chicago School of Law and Economics and the Scalia-Rehnquist-Thomas wing of the Court, the common law tradition is still capable of re-orienting legislative initiative.

Part One will trace the ascendancy of the takings clause and how it functions with respect to property. The takings clause is brought to bear to limit the legislature's power to pass regulation, serving to curtail the legislature's ambitions, that in effect takes, damages, or impedes private property. Chapter 1 presents a brief history of the origins of the takings clause. Chapter 2 takes up the post-Civil War developments in property law. Chapter 3 sketches out the modern criteria before taking or interfering with private property. Chapter 4 explains the Supreme Court's efforts to deal with the "compensation" and "public use" components of the takings clause. In the property law context, although the Supreme Court has yielded to the legislature the power to decide what constitutes a "public use" taking, it has not given up its power to decide how much compensation must be awarded for the taking. This will be expanded upon in chapter 4. Chapter 5 will examine the tension between the takings clause and the police power and the tests the Supreme Court spawned in dealing with the conflict. These tests are confusing because the common law approach to property and the regulatory agency approach can at times conflict. Also, the Court has been vague about the criteria that make up these tests. An understanding of the background development of these tests is important because it indicates the level of redistribution of property that the Supreme Court will allow from various legislative schemes.

The findings in the theoretical section of this work are as follows:

First, the position of postmodernist theorist, Minda, who does not take issues of predictability seriously, is mistaken. The postmodernist thesis of indeterminacy, with respect to predictability, is hard to defend. The ability to predict and generalize what the law *is* is a crucial and integral function of any rational legal system. On the point of predictability, Rose-Ackerman is correct to demand that legal decisions be constructed to allow for general and predictable statements of law.

Second, Radin's personality theory approach to property, in general and takings in particular, is neither realistic nor viable at this point in history. It just has little legal support, and market economists think it is unworkable. The differentiation she makes with regard to "fungible" property will not lead to "just" solutions. Although her sentiment is to achieve solidarity and community, the separation of property that she makes will not work to that end.

Third, the Coasean analysis of property is more persuasive than Peterson's moral presentation. Although ordinary people make moral judgments over regulatory takings affecting land use matters, this does not mean that they are right. The individual's moral perceptions or judgments may not be one and the same with the community's standards. Also, it is not clear from the history of land use management that the individual citizen's moral perceptions played much of a role in determining land use policy. The land use landscape seems to be more grounded on principles of "realpolitik" than moral judgments or perceptions. Although practitioners of realpolitik must be delicate not to offend citizens with their land use policies, moral judgment is not the basis of land use. From an analytic and substantive perspective, Peterson has not made a strong case for her moral principle.

Fourth, Michelman's utilitarian approach has some strong features. However, although this approach presents the best of all possible worlds in dealing with land use issues at the present time, it has a couple of very serious side effects. a) It violates the necessity for legal predictability. Because it relies too much on balancing tests, it presents outcomes that are less predictable than formalism or *per se* rules could otherwise achieve. b) This model forces Michelman to presents utilities and disutilities as if they can be accountable within a cost-benefit structure. But Michelman knows better. There are too many variables and intangibles that are not easily susceptible to measurement. As Fischel pointed out, cost-benefit analysis is more art than science. But at least it is a start. Michelman does recognize the limitations of utilitarianism and is prepared to use Rawlsian principles of "fairness" to ameliorate unjust utilitarian outcomes.

Fifth, although Sax presents a good case for more government intervention on behalf of ecological and environmental concerns, his approach is definitely tilted toward government intervention and biased against private property interests. He does well in presenting the high ideals of good environmental policy. However, he does not counterpoise those ideals with the equally important interests of people's right to obtain work. Clearly, there is a need for a political theory that can be informative as to how to deal with the concerns of environmentalists and property owners.

Sixth, modeling is an option if it could be worked out. However, Costonis's model is not viable as pointed out by Ross. At this time, a model cannot reflect accurately the judicial decisionmaking involving land use matters. Whether stable categories can be developed to give greater predictability of what the law is and at the same time render justice to the particular case remains elusive to modern jurisprudential theorists. The adoption of Costonis's model will lead to mechanical jurisprudence. Clearly, further work on this problem is necessary.

Seventh, the Scalia/Rehnquist return to the nineteenth century version of the common law is wrong. The exponential growth in industry, urbanization, and technology have undermined the rationality of the need to return to nineteenth century common law analysis. So it is impossible to go back to a century that gave the common law its individualistic character. Although there is still a need for the common law, it cannot be devoid of the developments of the twentieth century. So the Scalia/Rehnquist call for a return to common law principles is hard to defend because it is impossible to turn back the clock.

Eighth, the Chicago School of Law & Economics is too ideologically wedded to individualistic solutions to dealing with mass social problems. Although its market based economics has its virtues, it does not emphasize enough the problems of market failure—and not every social and legal problem can be addressed through markets. Epstein's and Paul's conservative and libertarian reading of takings law undermines modern civil society, by circumscribing and curtailing regulatory agencies to the most minimal level. Further, the grounding of law on natural rights jurisprudence is both wrong and misplaced, because the derivation of natural rights comes from a metaphysical base that is dated. This work argues that positive law is superior to the natural rights approach in dealing with property law.

Ninth, Sunstein presents a convincing case of why the regulatory state has not been a failure as is commonly believed in popular circles. It does not follow that an expansion of the regulatory state implies more bureaucracy. There is no reason why the modern state cannot deliver necessary services more efficiently, without the need to increase taxation, by leveraging the use of modern technology. Also, one should not be inclined to believe that market failure is not common. Nor should one believe that it is possible to turn over many state functions to markets. Property rights groups, however, are of the opinion that the regulatory state is too big as is and would slash and burn as much government as possible. This view is dangerous.

Tenth, Honore's view of 'ownership' is superior to Grunebaum's view that allows the object to drop out of the property relation. The word "property" has not become too metaphysical to serve its intended use. Although property should be viewed in relational terms, it is a mistake to view property as some "thingless" proposition.

What is clear is that the legal, economic, political, and philosophic dimensions to land use regulation will determine the space that is available for development in the twenty-first century. America is no longer a nation of vast open spaces. Our next frontier will be outer space than over the next hill. We cannot afford to use land as if we are still an open continent. As the continent fills up and becomes more crowded, there is a greater potential for escalation of disputes and violence over land use issues. So it is important that land use law be closely examined.

The property rights movement that is challenging us to dismantle most of the current Federal state needs to be answered. We need to respond as to why the minimalist state is not in the nation's best interest. These governmental minimalists overlook or forget one important axiom: our species is one of the most dangerous species to have emerged on this planet. This work takes the following proposition as axiomatic: the human species is the most barbarous and murderous species to have emerged on this planet. It is not only dangerous to its own kind but to every other species and, indeed, the planet itself. We cannot remove the restraint of government and also expect our species to revert to some utopian state of nature.

The political implication of this work is that our federalist structure of government imposes duplication costs that could otherwise be avoided under a unitary state. But if people want to maintain the Madisonian form of government, then they have to be prepared to pay for it. Madisonian government is not for the minimalists.

Under our form of government, the judiciary makes for a poor policy institution. When the other branches of government are deadlocked or have a thorny issue on their hands, they toss it to the judiciary. The judiciary cannot remedy the breakdown of civil society any more than it can resolve intense land use conflicts without direction from the elected bodies.

The judicial and political dimensions of land use are insufficient to deal with land use controls without some understanding of the economic and philosophical dimensions. Besides judicial determination, there resides the economic problem of valuations. This problem has vexed economists for some time. This work will not attempt to resolve such a foundational problem. The thorny problem is this: is the valuation of a thing/commodity a function of some intrinsic or inherent value of the property or is it based on subjective valuation of the good at the point of sale? The current assumption is that a good is not valued for some intrinsic aspect but based on the asked and accepted price. As indicated, the price/value gap will not be resolved here. Many economists tried to bridge the gap and failed. Yet it is an important matter in land use valuations because it goes to the issue of "fairness." If there is a taking of property, it would be fair, in setting the compensation award, to reflect its price/value. Currently, market price is the primary means of ascertaining value. However, the valuation that Wall Street places on a commodity leaves a lot to be desired. On Wall Street a commodity could lose half or all its value in a matter of seconds.

The philosophic premise that this work rests on should be stated up front. The current mapping of land has not been conducive to opening up social spaces for human growth. The carving up of the land and its markings has been mostly a function of economic determinations. This has created a social atmosphere that is detrimental to further economic prosperity and civil behavior. How the physical space is carved up plays an important role as to the type of social space that will emerge.

This work also presupposes a philosophic view of human nature that should also be stated up front. If the axiom is correct, that our species is a natural entity with dangerous instincts, then psychologisms are not the answer to social problems or legal determinations. Civil and legal problems should not primarily be resolved though talk therapies but through behavior modification. Problems of civil disintegration and individual criminal activity ought to be dealt with at the behavioral level. The need to discipline is not an outdated and barbarous practice, when the modern attitude is that anyone can do as they please, when they please, and for as long as they please without consequences. The ancients may have understood something about human nature and punishment that has eluded us. The substitute of psychologisms for discipline has resulted in a public state of affairs that threatens us all. Consequently, the grounding of this work rests on a view of human nature that is reformable through behavior modification rather than analysis. We have not evolved out of our brut status to be able to treat ourselves to the experimental positing of talk therapies, and the legal system should hold the line on overly relying on psychological factors in judicial determinations. The legal system is not the place to experiment with the latest psychoanalytic theories, since these theories rest on a rather dubious set of propositions. Consequently, judges should instruct juries to disregard or treat with a heavy dose of skepticism the theories of talk therapists. Such people may make good television entertainment but bad legal counselors.

This work will begin with some brief remarks on the origin of the takings clause. It will then proceed to lay out its post-Civil War development. After discussing the historical development of the clause, some major legal theoretical approaches will be discussed. It will be followed by an examination of the political, economic, and philosophic theories and implications of land use and property takings law, without any pretense of attempting to be exhaustive or comprehensive.

PART I

HISTORICAL ASPECTS OF TAKINGS LAW

CHAPTER ONE

ORIGIN OF THE TAKINGS CLAUSE

The origin of the takings clause is usually traced to the *Magna Carta*. Article 29 of the *Magna Carta* states that property must not be taken by the government except in accordance with the law of the land— "No freeman shall be [d]eprived of his freehold [u]nless by the lawful judgment of his peers and by the law of the land."[1] However, there is authority that traces it even farther back to the Roman period.[2] But the usual starting point is the *Magna Carta*, which only states that property will not be taken arbitrarily.[3] Even though this provision lacked a compensation component, it was an important first step in the protection of property from arbitrary confiscation.

Platt claims that, with the adoption of the *Magna Carta*, the thirteenth century marked "the dawn of the modern era of land use in England."[4] The erosion of feudalism would take many centuries to run its course. But the coming of the Industrial Revolution would precipitate not only economic, political, and social change, but also changes in law. The enclosure of the commons, along with demographic and technological changes, precipitated the need to change legal arrangements in order to accommodate post-feudal property concerns.[5]

The British colonies in America had the advantage of not being overburdened by tradition and history. In particular, the new geography made it difficult to duplicate feudal arrangements. Colonial property law in America did not replicate English feudal property law because the population was small and land was plentiful.

So even when there was a need to take private property in accordance with the law of the land, there was no need to fully develop a compensation provision for property taken. This was particularly true for property that was not developed. Treanor adds a political dimension to this general demographic and geographic explanation of takings.

> Neither colonial statutes nor the first state constitutions recognized a right to receive compensation when the government took property from an individual. Crown officials justified uncompensated takings by appealing to royal prerogative and limitations contained in original land grants. The absence of a just compensation clause in the first state constitutions accorded with the faith in legislatures that was a central element of republican thought and with the position held by many republicans that the property right could be compromised in order to advance the common good. (Treanor, p. 695).[6]

Treanor provides ideological reasons to explain early American reluctance to provide compensation for property takings. He points to republican ideology and faith in legislatures to do the right thing with regard to property rights. Treanor then claims that there was a loss of faith in republican ideals, which led to the inclusion of such clauses in state constitutions. The period he addresses runs from about 1776 to 1987.

> The Vermont Constitution of 1777, the Massachusetts Constitution of 1780, and the Northwest Ordinance of 1787 all required just compensation for governmental taking of private property. Adoption of these clauses evidences a growing rejection of traditional republican ideology, a decline of faith in legislatures, and a new concern for individual rights—particularly property rights. (Treanor, p. 701).[7]

It appears that Treanor wants to derive an ideological explanation for the addition of compensation clauses. However, this form of historical causation is difficult to prove. This is not to say that there is no connection between ideology and concrete transformations. There is a connection between ideas and activity. But the proof of the manifestation of that idea must reside in its actual manifestation and measured or observed in the physical world rather than in the heads of the participants. The point that is being made is that between the ideology and the manifestation there always exists problems of communication or miscommunication, and there is always a gap between theory and actuality. The prevailing ideology in 1776 may be one thing, its concrete manifestation another. Another example would be the Articles of Confederation. The theory of how this constitutional system was supposed to work and how in fact it did work illustrates that pure theory rarely matches reality in the day to day world of practical affairs.

Treanor goes on to elaborate the factors that led to these changes in the protection of property such as New York's interference with the property rights of New Hampshire settlers, after Vermont was given to New York, the confiscation of the property of loyalists, and the issuance of paper money that aided debtors over creditors. These are plausible factors, indeed. But are they sufficient to base generalizations upon? How could republican ideology account for these changes, before republican institutions could be developed. Republican institutions did emerge during the Revolutionary War. But, were they *real* institutions or seeds for the possible building of republican institutions? Reading Treanor, it appears as though the emergence of republican ideology entailed republican institutions popping up from nowhere, and within the span of a decade or so, were rejected.

Bosselman and Ackerman come closer to the truth of the matter. They conclude that the reason for the adoption of the takings clause, in general, to say nothing of the compensation provisions, has been imperfectly understood and not fully uncovered.[8] However, there is no doubt that the Framers of the Constitution wanted to place impediments to the taking of property. What steps were needed to be taken before interfering or taking private property were left for each State to decide.

Afterall, the Federal government had very few occasions to apply the takings clause after its adoption. A real need to apply such a provision did not manifest itself until well into the nineteenth century. This was so because the Federal government was small and its power limited, and the protection of private property could be achieved through the Contract Clause.[9] It should be remembered that, at the time, the protection of the Bill of Rights were applicable only to the Federal government and not to the States.[10] So during the close of the eighteenth century and much of the nineteenth, States adopted their own takings clauses and applied them as they saw fit, without supervision from the Federal judiciary.[11]

During the late eighteenth century and early nineteenth centuries, States took the lead in shaping their own land use policies; land use was (and still is) generally understood to be a local concern.

Horwitz believes that the judiciary played an important role in shaping the development of early American property law, and that the concept of property underwent a transformation during the early nineteenth century from what it was during the colonial period and late eighteenth century America. Horwitz claims that during the eighteenth century "the right to property had been the right to absolute dominion over land,"[12] and that this conception of property was "antidevelopmental" because it circumscribed neighboring property.

> As the spirit of economic development began to take hold of American society in the early years of the nineteenth century, however, the idea of property underwent a fundamental transformation—from a static agrarian conception entitling an owner of undisturbed enjoyment, to a dynamic, instrumental, and more abstract view of property that emphasized the newly paramount virtues of productive use and development. By the time of the Civil War, basic change in legal conceptions about property was complete. (Horwitz, p. 31).[13]

There are at least two difficulties with Horwitz's account so far—one is a minor qualification, the other more substantial. The minor point is his claim that prior to the nineteenth century individuals enjoyed absolute dominion over land. It would be more accurate to say that there never existed an *absolute* right to use one's property as one wished—as evidenced by the existence of the common law of nuisance. However, due to the spaciousness of the New World, one could act as if there were an absolute right to use one's property as one wished, in some instances.

The more substantial difficulty is that, according to Horwitz, the concept of property preceded the actual uses of this new development of property. Of course, logically it makes sense that the idea of property exits prior to its development. But what if history is not so clean cut or rational? What if history works the other way around; that there is trial and error, and then the idea crystallizes the substance of that discovery? That is to say, that there is no universal history or predetermined history. That history consists of the aggregation of happenings within the flow of time and space. The Hegelian notion of history as a movement of a predetermined and cyclical plan, moving dialectically, is more metaphysical than actual. It appears that history does not have a cyclical nature. Horwitz seems to be describing a set of events that have a certain developmental plan and form, capped off by judges acting in furtherance of said plan. History is messy and not only undetermined but underdetermined.

Horwitz's thesis is that property law was antidevelopmental during the eighteenth century. That is, a conception of property that was limited to its "natural uses"—meaning agrarian. And the "right of property" gave the owner who was there first the right to determine how the property was to be used—"first in time, first in right."[14]

Horwitz's conception of property is *instrumentalist*—meaning that it is used actively for the furtherance and expansion of capital, for the creation of wealth rather than maintaining the agricultural needs of the community. Property can be thought of as "dynamic/active," if it produces a return above the subsistence level. Otherwise, it is considered "static." Horwitz's thesis is that judges favored this active or instrumental use of property over the static use, leading judges to inject their own ideas of social policy into the law.[15]

Further, although there was a trend by States to add compensation clauses into their constitutions, indicating greater protection of property, Horwitz claims that there also existed a "countertrend to limit the scope of the application of compensation."[16] The countertrend was that judges provided less protection to property that was static.[17] Horwitz argues that although greater protection of property was provided through the addition of compensation clauses, there was, at the same time, instances where compensation was not actually made for damages,[18] since compensation was limited to "natural and proximate" causes and did not include consequential or indirect causes.[19] The next chapter will further develop the conditions that restricted compensation for regulatory takings and damages to property.

Despite Horwitz's tendency to a conspiratorial sense of history, he does present a coherent picture of early American property law. But, his theory of history, as developmental, is not justified. Even if judges favored this dynamic form of property over the static, there is no proof or evidence that they were consciously building a particular edifice.

This is not to say that new forms of property did not emerge during the nineteenth century. There did emerge new forms of property and property ownership. For example, the form and structure of modern corporations emerges during this century. Although the notion of a corporate entity is an old idea, its modern version bloomed in the nineteenth century. Horwitz's understanding of property can be profitably pursued as long as it is stripped of its bad metaphysics and his conspiratorial reading of early American history is viewed with a healthy dose of skepticism.

CHAPTER TWO

THE SHAPING OF THE AMERICAN STATE

A. *PHYSICAL INVASIONS*
B. *NUISANCE THEORY*
C. *POLICE POWER*
D. *SUBSTANTIVE DUE PROCESS*

The post-Civil War era brought about big changes in social and political structure wrought by war, industry, and demographics. The Supreme Court was at the forefront in helping to shape the new federalism. The Court assisted in transforming a nation of strong State and local controls, with a small Federal government, to one where the Federal government expanded and took jurisdiction over a greater area of interests that were previously considered the sole domain of the States. The Civil War was one of the major catalysts in the transformation of a nation of strong State control to a new federalism, in which the federal government consolidated its power and has since played an important role in overseeing State activity. However, the Federal government did not leap into the land use market directly. It was left up to the Supreme Court to freely make judicial policy as warranted. This has led to land use policies that are fragmented and *ad hoc*.

Curiously enough the Supreme Court legitimized greater federal involvement in the economy but the Federal government adhered, for the most part, to the idea that local government was the principal entity to set land use policy. And although the Court set broad rules for property takings, land use was not an area that the Court expended most of its energies on during this period of American history. This is not to suggest that that the Court's pronouncements were without effect. The shaping of the new-federalist constitution was brought forth through Supreme Court decision than legislative initiative. The legislature passed the Civil War Amendments, but it was the Supreme Court that shaped and interpreted them—especially its reading of the Fourteenth Amendment.

This chapter will give some sense of those changes as they affected land use and property law.

A. *PHYSICAL INVASIONS*

Prior to the Civil War, it was understood that interference with property meant the complete taking of the whole parcel. A new understanding, however, was emerging that did not simply see property as a physical thing but in a more abstract way. Property was starting to be conceived as an expectation or as a flow of income. Property did not have a fixed domain but a relational function that entailed more than its physical aspect. Land began its transformation from a physical entity to a capital one.

Up to the Civil War, and for many years afterwards, there was a general understanding of what a taking of private property entailed. It was generally understood that property was a material thing—a physical thing. The Supreme Court, in the *Slaughter House Cases*,[1] defined property as a physical thing—something with a "use value." But this definition did not last long because the dissent, in that case, put forth a different definition that would take hold in later years. The dissent defined property as having "exchange value."[2]

Sachman claims that there was a change in definition of property from "corporeal objects" to "exchange values."[3] This definition of property has important implications for takings law. Under the "use value" definition, it was not a taking if the property was not, strictly speaking, a "physical" object. For example, an interference with one's franchise could not, at this time, be considered a taking because franchises are intangible property rights. The definition used in the *Slaughter House Cases* would continue to be used in *Munn*. Sachman put it thus:

> "Property" in the popular ordinary usage, the usage of the common law, and the one adhered to in the *Slaughter House Cases* and in *Munn* case, means any tangible thing owned. "Property," in the later decisions, means any of the expected activities implied with regard to the thing owned, comprehended in the activities of acquiring, using and disposing of the thing. One is property in the sense of "things" owned; the other is property in the sense of "exchange-value" owned. One is represented by physical objects; the other, by marketable assets. (Sachman, p. 186).[4]

Sachman is making an important distinction. The implication of a taking under a physical invasion theory is that the whole thing must be taken before compensation is due. So if less than the whole interest was taken, then compensation is not warranted. But if property is defined as marketable assets or exchange value, a taking of less than the whole interest becomes compensable. The exchange value definition of property would later come to be known as the "bundle of rights" definition, which would encompass possession, use, and disposition. Each of these elements constitutes a stick in the bundle of rights. That is, property is not simply the fee (whole), but could be an interest that is less than the fee.[5]

Thus, it is possible to increase the number of takings by splitting property into parts and decrease the amount of compensation by paying only for the parts taken. This had been difficult when property was conceived of as a physical object.[6] "The doctrine that emerged from these cases was that property had to be taken in a physical sense, and then so completely as to amount to a fee interest, before the owner would be entitled to compensation. This doctrine of compensation prevailed throughout the period from 1824–1870."[7]

What the physical invasion theory of property entailed was that an interference that did not actually take title or possession of property (direct interference) was not a compensable taking. That is, indirect or consequential damage to property was not compensable. As mentioned in Chapter One, the Fifth Amendment was not yet applicable to the States. Although most States developed their own takings clauses, the application of these clauses was limited to direct physical invasions. In other words, the Federal government did not interfere with the States interpretation of their takings clauses.

The Civil War brought about the expansion of the Federal government. This expansion, of course, did not come overnight. It took many decades to work itself through—the culmination being the New Deal. There was an increased pace of industrialization and urbanization, which contributed to the growth of the Federal government. At first the Commerce Clause was used to expand its power and then other clauses were interpreted to consolidate a federal supervisory role over State activity. For example, the Federal government, prior to the Civil War, did not directly exercise its power of eminent domain.[8] If, for instance, the Federal government needed land to build a post-office, it would ask the State government to condemn the property.

But, with the case of *Kohl et al. v. United States*,[9] the Supreme Court put an end to this business of using the States as intermediaries and found that the federal government had its own power of eminent domain. The Supreme Court reasoned that if the States could exercise such power, it surely could not be denied to the Federal government.

By the end of the nineteenth century, the Supreme Court would deliver to the Federal government even more power, by interpreting the Fourteenth Amendment as incorporating the Fifth Amendment's taking clause. That is, the Supreme Court made the Fifth Amendment's Taking Clause limitations of interfering with private property applicable to the States. This meant that the Federal courts would exercise supervisory control over the application of each State's taking clause.[10] The case that made this interpretation or reading of the Constitution possible was *Chicago, Burlington & Quincy R.R. v. Chicago*.[11]

At first, during the 1870's, the Supreme Court adopted a physical invasion theory.[12] However, the Court, although working within the framework of physical invasion theory, began to expand the scope of compensation for physical takings.

As discussed in Chapter One, State courts were inclined to limit the range of application and the level of compensation for takings. The

Supreme Court extended the range of compensation with the case of *Pumpelly v. Green Bay Co.*[13] The Court ruled that indirect and consequential damage are compensable. The government raised a dam, which caused a lake to overflow and flood Pumpelly's land (640 acres). The overflow was *continuous* and worked a *complete* destruction of his land. The government argued that the damage was consequential and that the government had a right to improve navigable waters. The Court ruled for Pumpelly, even though the government did not take title or physical possession of the property. "[I]t remains true that where real estate is actually invaded by superinduced additions of water, earth, sand, or other material, or by having any artificial structure placed on it, so as to effectively destroy or impair its usefulness, it is a taking, within the meaning of the Constitutio[n]."[14] So *Pumpelly* modified the takings interpretation of not paying for indirect damages.

Pumpelly did not involve a taking of title or possession but a destruction of the "use" of property. This is an example of a case where taking one stick of the bundle of rights leads to compensation. This reading of property was not possible before *Pumpelly*. "A year after *Pumpelly*, the Supreme Court of New Hampshire handed down its decision in *Eaton v. Boston C. & M. R.R.* in which it explicitly relied on the bundle of rights conception of property and provided compensation for the taking of less than fee interests in property."[15]

This idea of compensation for consequential damages, however, has a very checkered and uneven development. The Court continued to uphold consequential damages as late as 1903, in the case of *United States v. Lynah.*[16] The Court in *Lynah* relied on *Pumpelly* to find a taking. The defendant's rice plantation was damaged because of the government building a dam across the Savannah River, and this caused the rice plantation to "become an irreclaimable bog, unfit for the purpose of rice culture or any other known agriculture, and deprived of all value."[17]

But the next year, in *Bedford v. United States,*[18] the Court retreated somewhat from its *Pumpelly* ruling. In this case, the Court found that a backup of flood waters, which was a consequential effect of government action, to be noncompensable. The Court said that there is a difference between damaging and taking. The Court distinguished *Pumpelly* on the ground the landowner in that case was *directly* injured by the dam project. In this case, the government had only reinforced the banks of the Mississippi River to prevent flooding, which was at a distant point from Bedford's land.

In the physical cases, the Court established a baseline that physical takings are compensable. However, this generally means that the damage is direct. The consequential or indirect effects of government action may be compensable, but would require a more careful examination of the facts. A strict reading of consequential damages could paralyze the government from taking action. This is the reason the Court wavered on awarding damages for consequential interference in private property.[19]

Despite the fluctuation, in these early physical invasion cases the Supreme Court set the stage for later development of compensation doctrine.

> The doctrine developed in *Pumpelly* and *Eaton* was not, however, immediately accepted. For example, in *Transportation Co. v. Chicago* and *Gibson v. United States* both *Pumpelly* and *Eaton* were characterized as extreme qualifications of the consequential damages doctrine, and distinguished as involving "a physical invasion of the real estate of the private owner, and a practical ouster of his possession," i.e., a virtual appropriation of title. Nonetheless, *Pumpelly* and *Eaton* stand as early examples of a line of cases more fully developed in twentieth century eminent domain and police power cases in which the concept of property was expanded through a recognition of intangible rights, the deprivation which required compensation. (Reznick, p. 868).[20]

Today, it is clear that the Supreme Court, through a long history of interpreting physical invasion cases,[21] considers such invasions as takings of property. And the Court has never retreated from this position in takings law. Due to the Court's consistency, there exists a very high predictability of the Court's position in such cases. However, as shall be seen in the next section, such consistency and predictability will vanish when the Supreme Court is dealing with regulatory takings.

B. *NUISANCE THEORY*

The previous section dealt with physical appropriations. This section will deal with regulatory appropriations. That is, instead of the physical destruction of property or its acquisition, regulatory interference of private property will be treated. Regulatory takings means the placing of limitations on the *use* of private property. The effect of the regulation is to render the property worthless or useless, in the more severe cases, although the owner still has possession of the property.

Nuisance is a common law remedy for dealing with infringements upon the enjoyment of one's property. It is individualistic in nature; problems are dealt on a case by case basis. The general common law maxim is: "use your property so as not to interfere with the use of another's property." A nuisance violation is considered a tort which means that there is a remedy in civil law for the infringement of an individual right.

Under nuisance theory, the government can extensively diminish the value of the tort-feasor's property. Under this theory what is central is that no one has a right to create a nuisance. In the pursuit of putting an end to the nuisance, the diminution in property value is not a central consideration. The case that best illustrates this point is *Mugler v. Kansas*.[22]

It is worthwhile to look more closely at this classic case because it places in perspective a body of legal thought that prevailed in late nineteenth and early twentieth century American law. Legislative bodies, under police power[23] authorization, can interfere with property that is detrimental to the community. In 1880 the Kansas constitution was amended to prohibit the manufacture and sale of intoxicating liquors in Kansas. The Kansas legislature, in 1881, pursuant to the constitutional amendment, passed a statute banning the manufacture and sale of intoxicating spirits. Mugler established his business as a producer and seller of beer a few years before passage of the amendment and legislation. Mugler based his argument on a violation of due process. Mugler essentially argued that the legislation had the effect of taking his property without compensation. Mugler's property, before the legislation, was valued at $10,000. After the legislation, it was valued at $2,000.

Mugler also argued that since he produced and distributed beer for export outside the state, the statute did not apply to his property. Furthermore, before the legislation, Mugler's activity was not deemed a nuisance. Yet, after the legislation, it *retroactively* became a nuisance.

The first Justice Harlan wrote the opinion of the Court. Justice Harlan read the takings clause literally. He said that no compensation was due because there was no physical taking, but only a regulation of property. Further, the State did not appropriate the property for its own use.

The first thing to notice about Justice Harlan's interpretation is that the word "take" is read literally.[24] The second thing to notice is that Justice Harlan sees property that is a nuisance to be a different "kind" than other physical property. So there is no need to consider the severity of the regulation on the value of the property. The diminution in value is irrelevant because the use that Mugler was putting his property to was a nuisance. The State *defined* it as a nuisance, and so it *was* a nuisance.

> [T]he early Supreme Court cases indicated that, despite severe economic damage to private property, there was no taking of property if there was a valid public purpose behind the challenged law and if there was no direct encroachment on the land. The classic case is *Mugler v. Kansas* where the test of a taking was refined slightly to become what was later described as the "benefit/detriment" distinction. (Large, pp. 8–9).[25]

The general principle that emerges from *Mugler* is that if the government is acting to prevent a harm or stop a nuisance, then there is no taking of property and hence no compensation. But if the government is not acting to prevent a harm but instead benefits or profits from the regulation, then there is a compensable taking.[26]

C. *POLICE POWER*

The police power began its ascendancy in the late nineteenth century, under the pressure of urbanization. As the problems of populated cities grew after the 1850's, it became necessary to expand "the traditional concept of common law nuisances into a general legislative authority, predicated on the police power, to regulate property in order to protect public health and safety."[27]

The police power is nowhere to be found in the text of the Constitution. It is understood to be a State's inherent power to regulate for the health, safety, morals, and welfare of its citizens.[28] It clearly is a broad power and its sweep is vast. It is generally said that government could not function without it or that the government would come to a standstill if it lacked such a power. The police power is presupposed or presumed to exit. Professor Freund noted, long ago, that this power eluded exact definition.[29] During Freund's writing of his classic book—*The Police Power*—limitations to the police power came through specific constitutional clauses such as contract or commerce.[30] Today, the takings clause provides some protection from police power regulation.

The use of the police power is generally understood to prevent harm. Because property can be put to uses that are detrimental to citizens, the government can through its police power regulate such activity. It is generally understood that there is no compensation forthcoming for regulation for the good of the community, even if it has the effect of taking or destroying someone's property. So the police power operates through regulations for the good of the community.[31] Professor Freund put it best when he said: "[I]t may be said that the state takes property by eminent domain because it is useful to the public, and under the police power because it is harmfu[l]."[32]

As stated above, the diminution in the value of property, under a police power regulation, is generally irrelevant. However, even Freund noted, as far back as 1904, that even if the police power action is lawful, it still should not reduce the value of property to zero. That is, under police power regulation, devaluations in property, are not of primary concern, but a regulation that *totally* wipes out all value is to be discouraged—that is, some value should be left over to the owner. "But the constitutional protection of property rights cannot in reason be satisfied by leaving the bare possession stripped of its economic value, and a prohibition of profitable use is to all intents and purposes a taking of property."[33]

That is, the regulation becomes too oppressive if it wipes out all value. This is not to say that, if need be, the value could not be totally destroyed. But Freund went on to say, in that extreme circumstance, the property value must be weighed against the public interest, and the public interest must be a strong one to justify destruction of property. He put it this way:

> The absolute destruction or abrogation of property rights—including confiscatory regulation leaving no reasonable profit to the owner—is an extreme exercise of the police power. Where it is proposed to exercise such authority, the constitutional right to private property must be weighed against the demands of the public welfare, and it is obvious that a public interest which is strong enough to justify regulation may not be strong enough to justify destruction or confiscation without compensation. Submission to regulation may be said to be one of the conditions upon which all property is held in the community; but total sacrifice negatives altogether the right of property. The conditions justifying the demand of such sacrifice must therefore be carefully examined. (Freund, pp. 550–551).[34]

As has been seen, *Mugler* allowed for severe reduction in property value. There is a case that allowed for even greater devaluation of property than *Mugler*. The case is *Hadacheck v. Sebastian*.[35] In this case, Hadacheck owned and operated a brickyard outside the city of Los Angeles. As the city grew, people started taking up residence near the brickyard. The city annexed the area. It took jurisdiction and passed legislation declaring the brickyard to be a nuisance, and under its police power stopped it from operating as a brickyard. The brickyard had a value of $800,000 before the legislation. After the legislation, its value was reduced to $60,000. The Supreme Court upheld the regulation.

Because the property is of a "kind" that is a nuisance, extreme value reductions are possible. Property, here, is not in "degrees." That is, it is not measured along a continuum. The "degree" taken is not considered.[36] Even though brickyards, stables, slaughter houses, etc. are not nuisances *per se*, they can become so under changed circumstances.[37]

The principle emerging is one where the police power is everywhere, and it takes a specific constitutional provision to mediate its effects. Of course, this does not explain how a use of property could at one point be tolerated and the next moment deemed a nuisance. The police power, however, is not only applicable or restricted to ending nuisances.[38] It can also be used in a positive way or proactively.

This raises the question of power. Who should ultimately have the power to determine what is and is not a nuisance? If the legislature says that X is a nuisance, could the judiciary reverse it? These are certainly difficult questions. Clearly, the legislature has the authority to declare certain activity a nuisance. And the judiciary has the authority to review the actions of the legislature.

A strict majoritarian count may result in arbitrarily taking property without some check by the judiciary. This leads to the classic dilemma as to whether unelected judicial officials have too much power in our democratic system. But, since the Constitution provides textual support for the protection of property, then the judiciary would be abdicating its duty if it did not see to it that the legislature obeys and follows the Constitution.

Although judicial interference can be viewed as working outside strict majoritarian principles, it nevertheless operates within a legal framework that has been sanctioned over time by the democratic process. If the judiciary abdicated its role as arbiter of reviewing what is a nuisance and whether compensation should be forthcoming, then the legislature would gain too much power and go unchecked. Under our system of checks and balances, the judiciary exists to prevent a "tyranny of the majority." Clearly, Justice Harlan would be inclined to defer to the legislature to determine what is a nuisance. However, whether he is prepared to give up the power of judicial review is unlikely. As will be seen in the next chapter, being more or less deferential to the legislature changes from Court to Court and doctrine to doctrine but giving up the power to have the last say is rarely conceded.

D. *SUBSTANTIVE DUE PROCESS*

During the late nineteenth and early twentieth centuries, the dominant clauses that the Supreme Court relied upon to strike down regulations that interfered with private property were the liberty of contract and substantive due process clauses. The takings clause was not at the forefront during this era. At times the Court simply lumped together due process and takings issues.

McGinley argues that the modern takings clause has its roots in the substantive due process doctrine.

> It is the Due Process Clause that was primarily used in the first 30 years of the 20th century by the Supreme Court to strike down legislation that "took" the value of private property as an incident to regulation of private conduct. This use of now discredited "substantive due process" analysis had its genesis in regulatory rate cases, such as *Munn v. Illinois*, and industrial regulation cases, including *Lochner v. New York*. Commentators who support

> this theory suggest that the source of confusion in constitutional "taking" analysis has been the judicially fueled doctrinal convergence and intertwining of the Due Process and Just Compensation/Eminent Domain Clauses. (McGinley, p. 344).[39]

The ruling in *Munn v. Illinois*[40] alarmed the business community due to this case's expansive reading of the police power.[41] The *Munn* case involved the regulation of grain elevators. Under the influence of the Grange movement, Illinois passed laws regulating the storage of grain. The Supreme Court allowed the State to regulate private property under the doctrine of property "affected with a public interest." The State argued that: by the nature of their work, these warehousemen, thrust themselves and their property into a class that rendered their property "affected with a public interest." Essentially, the State was saying that the warehousemen had established themselves as monopolists.[42] Justice Waite held that if there exists the power to regulate, there exists the power to set reasonable rates.[43]

The dissent in *Munn*, however, took exception to Waite's thinking and spelled out a doctrine that would emerge as the dominant view in due course. Justice Field, in dissent, said: "The principle upon which the opinion of the majority proceeds is, in my judgment subversive of the rights of private property, hencefore believed to be protected by constitutional guarantees against legislative interference, and is in conflict with the authorities cited in its support."[44]

Justice Field argued[45] that the Court misunderstood Sir Hale in its reference to him. When Sir Hale spoke about "property affected with a public purpose," he was speaking of public property, and the case before the Court only involved private property. That is, the state should not have exercised its police power because *Munn* involved private property and not public property. Justice Field, eager to protect private property, began searching for a clause that could best do the job. He found the due process clause.[46]

It took some time to transform the due process clause from its original procedural meaning into a substantive protection of private property.[47] The switch came with the case of *Chicago, Milwaukee, St. Paul Ry. Co. v. Minnesota*.[48] *Chicago, Milwaukee* argued that its rights were violated by having a commission set their prices.[49] Further, they argued that the legislature gave the power to the Commission to set rates as final without allowing for judicial review. The Court held that the legislature deprived the company of its property without due process of law. The establishment of a commission to set railroad rates amounted to a taking of private property. Although this case did not overrule *Munn*, it went a long way in crippling it.[50]

A search for a new clause to protect property was needed because legislatures continued using their police power authority to intrude on private property. Rate regulation could lead to other regulations that stripped property of most of its value.[51] Some way would have to be found to balance the police power of the State with the property interests of its citizens. Liberty of contract and substantive due process were brought to bear on the police power. *Lochner v. New York*[52] was the pinnacle of liberty of contract and substantive due process doctrine.[53] The worker's right to freely bargain with the employer trumped the State's right to mediate some of the harsh working conditions on behalf of the workers.

However, the dominance of liberty of contract would not last. By the late 1930's, it had run its course.[54] "Liberty of contract was effectively read out of the due process clause by redefining liberty in terms of those ends furthered by the police power of the state."[55]

What is clear is that the Supreme Court, and the judiciary in general, were not relinquishing their power. How did the Court managed to increase its power during this period? This is an interesting question. One theory as to how the Supreme Court accumulated such influence is that the Civil War effectively neutralized and disrupted the other branches of government. The Court was the only institution that was not reeling from the dislocation of the war experience, and during this period there was a window of opportunity for the Court to step into the space left open by the other branches of government. Although the power of judicial review was acknowledged long before the Civil War, in the post-Civil War period the Court managed to increase and consolidate its power. If we look at other European systems of government, they do not invest the level of power in their constitutional courts as we do in ours.

Physical invasions, nuisance theory, police power, and substantive due process played an important role in shaping constitutional law and the post-Civil War American state. As will be seen in the next chapter, Justice Holmes developed new theoretical tools for protecting private property.

CHAPTER THREE

THE BEGINNING OF MODERN TAKINGS LAW

A. *HOLMES & PENNSYLVANIA COAL*
B. *ZONING*

This chapter will discuss modern takings law. Modern takings law is grounded in utilitarian ethics. It received its shape in the hands of Justice Oliver Wendell Holmes. The thrust of this approach deals with balancing tests. Law is not derived from absolute criteria or metaphysics but rather shaped by the daily experiences of people. Consequently, absolute certainty and absolute justice are replaced with workable legal principles that are derived from the day to day life. Rather than viewing justice from a metaphysical frame of reference, i.e., natural law theory, utilitarian law theory is based upon a need to develop a workable methodology in the life as lived by citizens. Holmes would not dispense entirely with absolute justice or absolute right. But he would subordinate absolutism to arrive at a suitable and workable body of law that would weigh both ends of an issue or problem rather than turn to metaphysics for absolute and certain answers.

Utilitarian ethics forces judicial bodies to the use of balancing tests. This presupposes that there is a duality or plurality of positions that need to be considered before a final judicial determination is made. The utilitarian position cuts at theological positions that are neither susceptible to argument or alteration. This presumes that there is no single correct answer to a problem. A legal problem, if looked at closely enough, generates a multiplicity of options. The option that wins out may not have anything to do with being the correct, the beneficial, the right, the fair, or the just option. This raises the question: utility for whom? One man's utility is another man's burden.

As will be shown in this chapter, Justice Holmes stresses the *process* of balancing various interests rather than accept legal categories *a priori*. The outcome is secondary to the process. A utilitarian does not necessarily look for a "fair" outcome but a workable and pragmatic outcome.

A. *HOLMES & PENNSYLVANIA COAL*

Modern takings law was initiated by Justice Holmes with the 1922 landmark case of *Pennsylvania Coal Co. v. Mahon.*[1] Justice Holmes had been considering the problems addressed in *Pennsylvania Coal* long before he wrote this opinion. He started thinking about takings while serving on the Massachusetts Supreme Court. Justice Holmes had long been aware that if the police power were not restrained, then private property is gone. That is, if there is no limitation on the police power, the legislature is able to rapidly expand its power. The police power is so broad that at times it is viewed as being coterminous with government itself. Justice Holmes recognized the need to place some limits on such power.

Justice Holmes realized that the first Justice Harlan gave the police power a broad interpretation. If Justice Harlan's *Mugler* interpretation was taken as the standard, then the protection granted to private property would be greatly eroded. Now, Justice Holmes had no difficulty giving the legislature wide latitude to go about its business. Holmes's position was that elected representatives should have an opportunity to represent their constituents regardless of whether he agreed with their policies or not. Holmes clearly indicated this preference as far back as 1905, in his dissent in *Lochner*.

It would have been consistent, with his *Lochner* dissent, if Holmes had joined Justice Brandeis's dissent in *Pennsylvania Coal*. But he did not. He wound up writing the opinion of the Court—an opinion that some believe to be on a par with *Marbury v. Madison*; *Pennsylvania Coal* is to property and land use law what *Marbury v. Madison* is to judicial review. This is an opinion that has been cited no less than 100,000 times in the past 75 years. To say that this was a landmark opinion would underestimate its importance to modern takings jurisprudence. Some have gone as far as to claim that Holmes re-wrote the Constitution with this opinion.[2] Furthermore, after 75 years, this opinion is still good law and is still vigorously debated. Although some refinements have been made over the years, the basic principles of the opinion continue unaltered.

Justice Holmes did not hastily write this opinion nor briefly think about the issues involved. The Mahon's owned a house with a peculiar clause in the deed, though, perhaps, not so peculiar in the State of Pennsylvania. They owned only the surface estate. Pennsylvania law allowed for three different estates. The surface, support, and mineral estates can be viewed as separate estates. The Mahon's did not own the support estate nor the minerals (coal) underneath their house. These were owned by the Pennsylvania Coal Company. It can be assumed that the Mahon's or their ancestors contracted to buy the house, knowing full well that they were only buying the surface estate.

Since it usually took the coal company many years to reach one's property, one could enjoy the property for a long time before the company started mining operations. It was understood that: since the coal company owned the support estate, it would someday start mining the property. Hence, it would no longer be safe to live there due to the danger of collapse.

Pennsylvania became concerned about the safety of its residents from such cave-in problems and took steps to remedy the matter. Under its police power it passed the Kohler Act. This statute made it unlawful to mine under residential houses. Even though the company gave warnings as to when it would begin mining operations, Pennsylvania, nevertheless, believed it had the authority to pass this law.

The issue was phrased, as was the fashion of the time, in terms of due process and contract language. Should the State of Pennsylvania be able to abrogate the contract between Mahon and Pennsylvania Coal? The coal company certainly thought not. The company believed that its valuable property rights were being interfered with by the State legislature. Consequently, the company would lose profits if it desisted from mining under residential houses that contained similar clauses. The company claimed that the State took its property without compensation. Justice Holmes, writing for the Court, agreed with Pennsylvania Coal. Holmes believed that the legislature took valuable contract rights held by the company. The theories that came out of the case are: Property cannot be left without any reasonable use,[3] substantial interference with use—going "too far"—so as to diminish the value of property can be a taking,[4] balancing of interests, and average reciprocity of advantage.[5]

There was a clear trend toward the idea that a regulation that totally destroyed all value in property should be discouraged and therefore, should be declared a taking. Holmes clearly endorsed this position here. The diminution in value test is the critical test here because it transformed Justice Harlan's thinking about "kinds" of property into a quantitative (or "degree") of interference standard. The balancing of interests test shows Holmes's utilitarian-pragmatic philosophy. Finally, the average reciprocity of advantage test was discussed but was not determinative in the case. This test involves looking to see if the burdened party benefits in any way from the regulation. All of these tests go to use rather than possession of property. As we have already seen, if government takes possession of property, it leads to compensation. Here, we are dealing with regulations that interfere with the uses of property.[6]

Pennsylvania Coal recognized that absolute and inflexible criteria for property takings had serious consequences for property owners. Holmes hoped to mediate this effect on property by offering a balancing of interests test. That is, he sought to modify Justice Harlan's literal interpretation of property takings with a utilitarian-pragmatic approach.[7] Justice Harlan considered the quality of the taking (e.g., whether nuisance or not). Justice Holmes considered the quantity of the taking.[8] Presumably, the higher degree of interference, the more likely there is a taking. The difficult question, of course, becomes how much regulation is too much? Holmes left that question open.

Holmes's basic concern was to place a limit on the level of interference of private property that a legislature should be allowed without compensating the owners. Holmes's utilitarian approach entailed balancing the government's need to regulate the use of property against the interests of owners. In Mahon's case, the private interests of leaving their house standing were balanced with the coal company's valuable bargained for contract rights.[9]

Furthermore, we need to take note of what was taken here. The facts indicate that the support estate was taken. How much was taken? The facts indicate 100% was taken. This is important because it answers the question of whether there was a diminution in value. For example, if only one-third of an estate were taken, then it would be less likely to be a diminution in value severe enough to warrant finding a taking. But if 100% of the estate was taken, then compensation should be forthcoming.

How were courts to decide whether one of three estates were taken or all three estates? Justice Holmes looked to Pennsylvania law. Since Pennsylvania allowed for the existence of three independent estates, then the whole (support) estate was taken. Hence, this was a confiscation of private property. Of course, Holmes left us with the bigger problem of deciding how far is "too far" in the diminution of value. His theory only suggests that the higher the degree of interference, the higher the risk the regulation is a compensable taking.

The final test mentioned in *Pennsylvania Coal* is the average reciprocity of advantage test. That is, if a regulation benefits the burdened party, then this should be considered as to whether compensation should be made. *Plymouth Coal Co. v. Pennsylvania*[10] was the case that Holmes cited as precedent for *Pennsylvania Coal* on the meaning of this test.[11] Coletta claims what is distinct about— *Plymouth*— is that the benefits accrued from the regulation were indirect and did not benefit the immediate party (the party that bore the regulation).[12] Coletta believes that this test should be read broadly. That is, as long as the regulation benefits the community as a whole, it does not matter whether the particular owner, whose property is burdened by the regulation, benefits or not.[13] However, such a reading would undermine the other tests. Holmes himself would not give this test a broad reading. A fair reading of this test might be: if the regulation benefits the burdened owner, then this should be considered in the reduction of the compensation award and not serve in place of compensation. However, this test was noted in *Pennsylvania Coal*, but not used there, because the "burdened party (Pennsylvania Coal) did not receive any benefit."[14]

> *Pennsylvania Coal* clarified the parameters of the concept of average
> reciprocity of advantage by requiring that tangible, albeit sometimes indirect,

benefits result to the regulated parties. The burdened individual must receive some distinct benefit not enjoyed by the community as a whole. (Coletta, p.322).[15]

Justice Brandeis, in his dissent, took up the traditional nuisance reasoning developed by Justice Harlan.[16] Brandeis claimed nuisance activity could not be protected or shielded by contract law. Contract law is insufficient to protect property deemed to be harmful to the community. "Changed circumstances perhaps increasingly intensive mining (though Brandeis did not specify), can make a once harmless use noxious. Private individuals cannot remove an activity from the reach of the police power by means of a grant or contract, nor can the state bargain it away."[17] Holmes thought otherwise. Although the police power can be used to safeguard the health, safety, morals, and welfare of the community, Justice Holmes realized that such power can be used as a short cut to takings of private property without compensation—basically as a means of redistribution. "We are in danger of forgetting that a strong public desire to improve the public condition is not enough to warrant achieving this desire by a shorter cut than the constitutional way of paying for the change."[18]

Why did Holmes, usually open to legislative initiative, quash the legislation here? McGinley claims that he did not mean to do so.[19] McGinley is trying to soften the impact of *Pennsylvania Coal*. He thinks the limitations placed on the police power were an aberration.[20] This reading is unwarranted because, as indicated in earlier chapters, the thrust was building to do something about an unlimited police power, and fragments of these theories and tests were flowing around many years before *Pennsylvania Coal*.

The effect of Holmes's interpretation of the taking clause was to bring government to a median point, where the legislature was not given absolute power through a limitless police power. At the same time, the legislature was not so weak that it could not function because of having to pay for the slightest intrusion, regardless of how *de minimis* the taking. Thus, the effect of Holmes's balancing test is to limit government, by having it pay compensation where its regulations are confiscatory or severe. So, if the legislature wanted to increase its taking of private property, it would also be forced to increase taxes or borrowing to pay for it.

B. ZONING

Zoning is a statutory means by which to control land use. Zoning, as opposed to the common law, is legislative control over land use. The States have what are known as "enabling statutes" that authorize local governments to pass zoning laws.[21] Municipalities have no inherent authority to pass zoning laws unless there exists an enabling law that authorizes them to zone—the power to zone rests with State governments and not its subdivisions. But, it is local governments that do the actual zoning, not the State.

Williams and Taylor break up zoning into five periods.[22] The first period covers the first two decades of the twentieth century. These early zoning laws basically divided a community into three districts: residential, commercial, and industrial. This basic pattern continues to exist today. It has become more complex, with greater refinements in the classification structure. But the principle of splitting up the community, to exclude incompatible uses of land, is still followed. Land use controls of this sort were usually found to be unconstitutional during the first period.

The second period begins with Supreme Court approval of zoning in 1926. During this period, following *Euclid v. Ambler Realty Co.*,[23] two principles were established.

> [P]rivately owned land could be made subject to broad restrictions on its uses, without compensation, and the uses of land could be arranged into district[s]. [I]n this stage the courts suggested, somewhat hesitantly, that the power to regulate the physical environment extended beyond the power to control nuisance[s]. (Williams & Taylor, p. 105).[24]

Usually, land use laws were held valid during this period.

The third period started in most states during the 1950's and 1960's. Courts went to the other extreme, by upholding most of what States passed, favoring local zoning boards over private interests. Courts generally gave great deference to local zoning bodies.[25]

The fourth period started around the 1970's, with courts attempting to balance the various interests. That is, there was a more genuine and realistic balancing of special interests against government objectives.

The fifth period started in 1986 requiring mandatory damage remedies and a shift back to a more cautious stage—the second stage. This stage running roughly from 1930 to 1950.[26]

The need for zoning arose because the common law of nuisance was not adequate to deal with modern problems of urbanization and industrialization, nor could it adequately protect private property from incompatible uses. The common law of nuisance was sufficient for an agrarian society, where distance allowed property owners to avoid most of the effects of incompatible uses.[27]

During the pre-zoning period, legislative attempts to deal with land use problems, outside the framework of the common law, led to invalidation of such laws.[28] As long as legislatures passed land use laws within the limits of the common law, the courts were amenable to police power intrusions on private property as mapped out by that framework.[29] As already discussed, police power takings were not unlimited, even under Justice Harlan's reading of the takings clause. "It seems quite clear that following *Euclid,* the required relation to the police power could be established without a demonstration that a proscribed use was either a nuisance in the common law sense, or something closely analogous to a nuisance."[30]

The case that legitimized zoning, or, constitutionalized it, was *Euclid v. Ambler Co.*[31] This case is the basis for modern zoning law. The Village of Euclid, an Ohio municipality, was practically a suburb of Cleveland. It had a population between 5,000 and 10,000 and had an area from 12 to 14 square miles. It was mostly farm land and unimproved. Ambler Realty bought 68 acres of land. On. Nov. 13, 1922, the Village Council adopted a law establishing a comprehensive zoning plan.

Ambler Realty owned the land before the enactment of zoning laws and intended to sell it for industrial purposes. That is, it was in the path of development. The land was valued at $10,000 per acre if developed for industrial purposes, and its value dropped sharply if restricted to residential uses. Its residential value was $2,500 per acre.[32] The ordinance classified Ambler's land as residential. Ambler Realty argued that these laws deprived them of their property in violation of due process. The Supreme Court held the ordinance was reasonable and not arbitrary.[33] The zoning plan was upheld, despite the devaluation of property.[34]

Land use issues would be abandoned by the Supreme Court from roughly the late 1920's to the early 1970's.[35] *Nectow v. Cambridge*[36] would serve as the last case before the Court left this area. *Nectow,* basically, served to limit reading *Euclid* broadly. Again, this was a due process complaint. Before passage of the zoning ordinance Nectow contracted for the sale of his land for $63,000, but due to changes in zoning restrictions, from industrial to residential, the buyer refused to comply with the contract. The Supreme Court overturned the zoning classification as applied to Nectow's property because the locality was more suitable for "industrial uses rather than residential."[37]

The importance of *Nectow* is to limit zoning to the context of the particular environment. And if the zoning is arbitrary, then the litigant can obtain an exception from the zoning law.

> The governmental power to interfere by zoning regulations with the general rights of the land owner by restricting the character of his use, is not unlimited, and other questions aside, such restrictions cannot be imposed if it

does not bear a substantial relation to the public health, safety, morals, or general welfare.(*Nectow*, p. 188).[38]

Basically, the 1920's set the stage for modern means of regulating land use and takings criteria. What the Supreme Court gives with one hand it takes with the other. *Euclid* and *Nectow* illustrate this. *Euclid* authorized zoning but *Nectow* gave the Supreme Court the final power to decide if those zoning laws are in conformity with a given environment. As previously indicated, the power of judicial review is rarely given up by the Court. The power struggle between the Supreme Court and the legislature does not always surface. But land use is a contested area and the struggle between the two bodies at times breaks the surface.

It was shown that Justice Holmes, following in the American tradition of pragmatic philosophy, attempted to balance the competing interests rather than rely on categorical rules. Formal rules are insufficient to accurately grasp the flow of time and circumstance, in contrast to utilitarian principles which can. Certainly, Holmes would have felt very uncomfortable laying down the law *a priori* rather than exploring the issues from both sides of the equation. In this sense, Holmes is a forerunner to Ronald Coase. Later chapters will develop how Coase would look at takings law.

Zoning developed as an alternative to the common law tradition. It did not fit comfortably in a framework that particularized social problems at the individual level. Mass solutions to individual needs and mass production become the standard-bearers of the Industrial Age. The individual does not take priority, in the age of the production line. Masses of individuals cannot be treated as unique with tailor made solutions to their problems. Courts ultimately recognized that in order to obtain the benefits of mass production, something had to be exchanged for them. If factories cannot be placed at optimal locations, then individuals could not expect to enjoy the level of material satisfaction of the goods produced at a reasonable cost. Clearly, most citizens preferred to have more material goods than cleaner environment at that point in history. So what if their neighborhood or community was covered in soot? In the utilitarian universe, trade-off and balancing of interests dominate the perspective of its inhabitants.

Nuisance law, under industrialization, can be a tiresome examination of case by case complaints in a universe that was eclipsed by the machine. The pastoral setting of nuisance law came into contact with a world that operated under a different logic. The logic of the machine age is different from the logic of the horse and buggy universe. In the utilitarian calculus the change in universe is taken as given. Then the utilitarian question becomes do we protect property as we did in a pastoral setting or do we adjust to the new environment?

The courts usually trail in these determinations. They do not set the pace nor the agenda for change, in most cases. When courts move to the forefront, they usually serve as endorses of change that is already under foot rather than as initiators of change. Changes in social policy brought forth by courts are not done in some conspiratorial sense or *a priori* but as a recognition that circumstances have changed. The courts did not go about favoring factory interests over communities covered in soot. Noise and pollution are the byproducts of the Age of Industry. The utilitarian calculus simply recognizes what *is* the case rather than what should be the case.

CHAPTER FOUR

THE SUPREME COURT ABANDONS LAND USE LAW

A. GENERAL EXPLANATION
B. JUST COMPENSATION (CONDEMNATIONS)
C. PUBLIC USE (CONDEMNATIONS)
D. GOLDBLATT CASE

Despite Justice Holmes's efforts to deal with takings issues, the complexity of the land use takings problem requires more than balancing interests. Holmes established tests that lack precision and rigor. Consequently, they became open ended and subject to countless interpretations. Furthermore, Holmes left courts with the problem of determining where along his continuum the balance tips in favor of a particular plaintiff. These problems have continued to plague takings law to the present. Holmes is not to be criticized because he was balancing interests. Rather, the tests he used were very loose and the framework was so open-ended that it gave little concrete guidance to future courts as to what to do. Of course, it must be remembered that the Supreme Court is not solely to be blamed for the outcome in takings law. The States and the Federal government relegated land use oversight and responsibility to local governments and municipalities.

This work takes the position that local government should not be the sole guardian of land use policy. Not simply because they are susceptible and vulnerable to special interests, since this is a malady that can afflict all levels of government and all branches of government. But because their primary interests are mainly concerned with their own territory. If the proposition is correct that people privilege their own locality, customs, and traditions, then it becomes clear that this type of parochialism can be detrimental to the broader community. There is nothing wrong with pride of place, but if this is defended at all costs, then it leads to a narrow and limited outlook on life. This is and has been, if history is to teach us something, a critical source for bloodshed. Animals defend their territory and well they should. It takes real effort for animal behavior to be modified. If each community privileges its own interests, then we are all worse off in the long run because neighboring communities will turn on each other during hard times if there is no greater interest or power to stop them. In the international arena states turn on neighboring states first. The same principle is applicable within the state. Neighboring communities will be at each others throats if there is no greater state to step in during difficult times.

The Supreme Court abandoned land use issues. One reasonable and foundational explanation is that: since it was presumed and implicitly understood that localities know what is best for them, they should be left to their own devises in dealing with their own land use and takings problems. This more or less is the position of all the other higher level bodies of government. This chapter will sketch out additional reasons than can help explain the Court's absence from the land use field. It will be followed by an examination of the "just compensation" and "public use" provisions of the takings clause. During this period the Court attempted to clarify the constitutional limitation of these provisions in the analysis of property problems. The chapter will close with an analysis of a major land use case of the period.

A. GENERAL EXPLANATION

By the close of the 1920's the Supreme Court abandoned land use cases with a few exceptions, for approximately the next forty years. The Court would not re-assert its authority over land use issues until the 1970's. This, of course, does not mean that land-use law came to an end. What happened was that each State continued to develop its own land use law. Also, this is not to say that during this period the Court abandoned takings law itself—only takings as applied to land use. Takings occurring outside of land use were regularly dealt with. Cases, for example, dealing with capital goods, such as factories, were taken under condemnation law.[1] Furthermore, during this period, the Court clarified its interpretation of "just compensation" and "public use" provisions of the takings clause.

Here are some of the reasons that may help to explain the Court's absence from the field.

First, land use is taken to be a local matter, and the best place to review related legislation is in the state courts. The Supreme Court may have reasoned that land use is a State and local concern. There is a tradition that the best government is one that is closest to the people. Therefore, land use supervision should be left to State courts and allow local authorities to deal with their own land use problems.

Second, the Depression hit in the 1930's, and President Franklin D. Roosevelt's New Deal agenda challenged the Supreme Court to abandon some of its interpretations of the Constitution and common law understanding of property law. The Court was also put under severe pressure from President Roosevelt to be more amenable to his New Deal legislation. President Roosevelt threatened to expand the number of justices that can sit on the court. Due to pressure, retirements, and a switch in vote by Justice Roberts, the Court yielded to the demands of Roosevelt. This change in Court configuration, also, brought a change in doctrine. It brought to an end "substantive due process" judicial review and the end of the "liberty of contract" doctrine. The Court, basically, abandoned vigorously reviewing economic/property legislation. Of course, this does not mean that no judicial review was available—but, only minimal review was available, which is very deferential to the government.[2] So the Supreme Court may have been taught the lesson that majoritarian politics cannot be ignored entirely and consequently, became more circumspect in boldly standing in the way of mass coalitions and groups that are bent on reading the Constitution their way.

Third, the Second World War broke out. The Court was busily engaged in assessing compensation issues, due to government re-direction of private capital such as condemnation of factories, mines, and other capital equipment, in order to prosecute the war.

Fourth, the Civil Rights movement in the 1950's and 1960's re-focused the Court's attention from economic/property concerns to civil rights/liberties concerns. The Court became more activist in the civil rights arena, especially under the leadership of Chief Justice Earl Warren.

And, finally, what may have compelled the Court to return to land use issues in the 1970's is that the effects of industrialization and urbanization were not going away. The rise of the Green Movement—environmentalism—and new scientific findings concerning ecology, all may have contributed to re-focus the Court's attention to land use concerns.

B. *JUST COMPENSATION (CONDEMNATIONS)*

The Just Compensation provision of the Constitution is one area where the Supreme Court attempted to come to grips during this period (1930–1970) with what these two words entailed. The best way to find out what "just compensation" means is to look at Supreme Court cases involving condemnations, because in such cases the main issue is compensation. As already pointed out in the previous chapter, compensation generally serves as a deterrent to the taking of property, by an overly zealous legislature.

The first thing to note is that subjective valuation of property is generally not allowed in determining compensation. Just compensation is based on market value. Exceptions are possible but are not the norm. In condemnation cases, the government's authority to take property is usually conceded. The central question, then, is how much must the government pay? A condemnation proceeding is one where the government, pursuant to eminent domain authority, takes private property.

The usual formula for compensation awards generally involves the physical taking of property, and valuation is based on the physical thing taken—e.g., the land was flooded, the improvements on the land were destroyed, etc. But late in the nineteenth century, the Court determined it is not only possible to take physical assets, but a taking of intangible assets is also possible—e.g., bonds, stocks, franchises. An early nineteenth century case that set the parameters of the compensation package for condemnations was *Monogahela Navigation Co. v. United States*.[3] In 1836, the State of Pennsylvania authorized the Monogahela Navigation Company to build dams. The Monogahela River was not navigable by large ships, without lock and dam improvements. Before these improvements were made, the river was only able to accommodate small tonnage ships and only during certain times of year. But, now, due to the locks and dams constructed by Monogahela Navigation, large tonnage steamships can be accommodated. Monogahela Navigation had expended large sums of money to make these improvements.

The question in the case did not turn on whether the government had authority to condemn the locks and dams. This much was conceded by the company. The issue was how much must the Federal government pay to condemn the property? The government wanted to pay for only the physical improvements—such as the locks and dams. Monogahela Navigation, however, wanted the government to pay also for taking its franchise to collect tolls. This franchise was valuable property. The Court held for Monogahela Navigation. The Court basically said that the legislature may decide whether to take property or not or what property is needed by the public. These are legislative questions. But when a taking has occurred, how much the government must pay cannot also be a legislative question. What is just compensation is a judicial question.[4]

The Court valued property on its productiveness rather than just its physical plant or fixed assets.[5] So it is not simply the construction—bricks and mortar—that determines the value of property but what the "completed structure brings in to its owner."[6] The Court said:

> There were the franchises of the company, including the right to take toll, and these were as effectively taken as was the bridge itself. Hence, to measure the damages by the mere costs of building the bridge would be to deprive the company of any compensation for the destruction of its franchises. The latter can no more be taken without compensation than can its tangible corporeal property. (*Monogahela*, p. 329).[7]

What is included in the compensation package depends on the nature of the takings.[8] The case that best explains what is included in a compensation package is *United States v. General Motors Corp*.[9] This is a World War II period case, where there was a temporary taking of a lease. This case makes clear that market value is the basis for compensation, and intangible assets (such as leases) must be included in the compensation award. It, also, specifies what is not included in the compensation award. For example, there is no compensation for consequential costs; there is no compensation for loss of future profits; there is no compensation for moving removable fixtures and personal property; there is no compensation for loss of good-will; and there is no compensation for consequential costs in relation to moving and relocation.[10]

Thus, just compensation means minimum compensation or "no frills" compensation. One is entitled to compensation for the physical or intangible asset, but anything in relation to or surrounding the basic item or product is excluded. Whether this is what the Bill of Rights means by "just compensation" is another matter. So it appears that although the government must pay something, that something appears to be the low end of the range of damages that could have been compensated. Further, *General Motors Corp.* stands for the proposition that government cannot take an asset—chop off the portion that it needs—and then only pay for what it took, regardless of whether it has devalued the rest of the asset.[11]

Another case that affirms that consequential costs are not compensable and only assets that have exchange value are compensable is *Kimball Laundry Co. v. United States*.[12] The U.S. Army condemned a laundry plant and used it for its own purposes. The issue was whether to include payment for damages to the trade route—a list of customers the company had built up over the years or "good will." Justice Douglas, in dissent, could not understand why "good will," which is not compensable for permanent takings, was included in the award for temporary disruptions of business. As already indicated, only exchange value was compensable,[13] so what exchange value could be placed upon trade routes that were of no value to the Army? Although trade routes are useless to the Army, they are still valuable interests to the property owner. Justice Frankfurter writing for the Court basically said that trade routes resulted from the superior skill in "management and more effective solicitation of patronage than are commonly given to such a combination of land, plant, and equipment."[14] The Court awarded money for the loss of trade routes.[15]

The gist of these cases is compensation will be forthcoming for condemnations, but what is included in the award is a contested matter and usually involves the narrowest understanding of what the compensation award entails rather than full compensation for all intended and unintended consequences of the condemnation.

C. PUBLIC USE (CONDEMNATIONS)

Understanding the Public Use provision of the Constitution is helpful in better understanding the history of takings law. The Supreme Court during this period (1930–1970) gave some important clues in setting the parameters of this constitutional provision.

What is meant by "public use?" The "public use" component of takings has had an uneven existence. At one time the clause was read narrowly, at other times broadly, and currently is almost irrelevant in takings jurisprudence. But because it is in the text of the Constitution and since there are multiplicity of Supreme Court interpretations of the clause, many theorists see the current Supreme Court's neglect of the provision as being irresponsible in correctly reading the Constitution. That is, the Supreme Court has read this clause out of the Constitution. Under a narrow reading, it means "use by the public." Under a broad reading, it means "public benefit."

> As was the case with the public use limitation in state condemnations, the Supreme Court in dealing with the federal condemnations did not make an early choice between the "use by the public" test and the broad public benefit theory. The early federal takings were for activities which could have withstood the rigors of the "use by the public" test, such as parks and national monuments, and therefore, a choice was not essential. In later years, however, it became apparent that federal takings were not being subjected to the "use by the public" test but were to be upheld if they were beneficial or advantageous to the public. (Comment, p. 610).[16]

The lead case in the modern interpretation of "public use" is the urban renewal case, *Berman v. Parker*.[17] This case involved the constitutionality of the 1945 District of Columbia Redevelopment Act. Congress declared it was the policy of the United States to eliminate all substandard housing in Washington, D.C. because such structures were a threat to public health, safety, morals, and welfare. The Act created the District of Columbia Redevelopment Agency, and granted the Agency the power of eminent domain to take property in blighted areas for redevelopment purposes. Berman owned a department store in this redevelopment area. Berman argued that his property was commercial rather than residential, and it was not slum housing. He further argued that because the redevelopment was for "private" use, it violated the takings clause's "public use" provision. The redevelopment would benefit other private interests rather than the public at large. The Court upheld the legislation.

The significance of this case is that the "public use" requirement is to be read broadly.[18] Ellen Frankel Paul says this means that once the legislature has decided that a certain property is for "public use," then the Court will defer to legislative judgment.[19] Paul, however, suggests the Court was not always so liberal in its reading of the clause. She argues that Justice Black was one of the principal architects in crippling this clause. "Justice Black went a long way toward removing the Court from being the final arbiter over the question of public use."[20] Paul believes that there ought to be a more stringent examination to government takings, and this could come from using the "public use" provision to cut down on non-emergency or non-essential governmental invasions into private property, regardless of whether they are compensated or not.

The impact of *Berman* is it removes a constitutional limitation of subjecting government takings to a narrow interpretation of the clause.

> If the legislature is "well-nigh" the final arbiter of "public use," who will protect private rights? The Court apparently lost sight of one of the principal purposes behind the Fifth Amendment's property clause: to protect private property owners by limiting governmental confiscation of property to those instances in which an overriding public necessity made the taking necessary. This is the whole point behind the public use proviso. (Paul, Ellen Frankel, pp. 363–364).[21]

Bender takes a different approach to this problem. She claims there has been a conflation of due process and "public use" analysis. That is, the due process "public purpose" limitation was imported over to the public use provision in takings issues.[22] This is wrong, according to Bender, because due process limitations only receive rational basis judicial review and that such review should not apply in the taking of property because it has its own constitutional/textual provision.[23]

Fawcett also thinks that after *Berman*, it is no longer sensible to question the legislature on this point. "Implicit in the application of this view to the area of eminent domain is the notion that the right to be free from uncompensated takings is not so fundamental as to require strict judicial scrutiny."[24]

What these theorists are basically saying is that the Supreme Court has come to the conclusion that it should not meddle too much with the will of the legislature over public use questions.

> Today, the eminent domain power, as a legitimate means, has been expanded enormously beyond its early boundaries. Indeed, the government's power of eminent domain has become so broad that it is now said to be coterminous with the scope of the sovereign's police power. "Public use" has come to mean in furtherance of the public interest in health, safety, welfare or morals, and the decision regarding what constitutes these ideals is left to the legislature. Most courts, although empowered to decide questions of public use, choose not to second-guess the legislature. Thus, the early real protection of the private property owner against an unwise or expansive exercise of eminent domain is monetary—the payment of just compensation. (Fawcett, p. 499).[25]

Furthermore, Dunham thought that the "use by the public" test at least had an objective ring to it. In that, within limits, it was possible to determine whether an appreciable amount of the public would use the property. He also suggested that such a test privatized values. If the condemnation did not benefit the public—was not used by the public—then it was best that the government stayed out and allowed markets to deliver the services.[26]

Dunham believes that the containment of legislative power provided by the "public use" limitation was dying long before *Welch* (an earlier case dealing with the problem of how to read the public use provision) and *Berman*, but these two cases ended any meaningful review by the Supreme Court.[27] "By freeing the legislature from an inability to pay compensation for a restriction on use of property even where the legislature thought it just to do so, these two landmark cases, *Welch* and *Berman*, enlarged legislative responsibility."[28]

What we have here is a shift in power as to who decides "public use" questions. The *Berman* decision effectively took the judiciary out of the public use business.[29] Perhaps, the Court was still reeling from its 1930's battle with the other branches of government over liberty of contract. Its interpretation of "public use" doctrine is an instance of deference the Court showed the legislature. The Court was deferring to the democratization process rather than applying the special protection of the Bill of Rights against majoritarian intrusions on private property. It appears that the 1950's was not a good decade to re-stage the battle over economic/property issues.

D. GOLDBLATT CASE

Goldblatt v. Town of Hempstead[30] is an example of those rare cases during this period (1930–1970) in which the Supreme Court addressed land use concerns. This case is an early indication of the difficulties the Supreme Court will encounter in providing workable tests to deal with land use problems. Goldblatt owned a 38 acre tract in the Town of Hempstead. The Town took legislative action to stop Goldblatt from operating a sand and gravel pit until he obtained a permit. Goldblatt had used his property for mining sand and gravel continuously since 1927. Because of continuous excavation, the company had reached the water table and the pits would fill up with water. So part of his property had become a lake.

The town expanded around the excavation within a radius of 3,500 feet. In the area there were more than 2,200 homes and four schools.[31] Goldblatt's property was not a nuisance *per se*, but his excavating activity became incompatible with the surrounding town. So the Town passed an ordinance prohibiting him from further excavation. Goldblatt argued the ordinance was not just regulatory but confiscatory. It negated previous court judgments in his favor. Further, the ordinance, claimed Goldblatt, was an *ex post facto* law.[32] He lost his case in the New York courts and appealed to the Supreme Court. The Court found the ordinance lawful. It said:

> Concededly the ordinance completely prohibits a beneficial use to which the property has previously been devoted. However, such a characterization does not tell us whether or not the ordinance is unconstitutiona[l]. If the ordinance is otherwise a valid exercise of the town's police powers, the fact that it deprives the property of its most beneficial uses does not render it unconstitutional. (*Goldblatt*, p. 989).[33]

What is clear from this case is the Court was unwilling to provide specific criteria for police power action. This case foreshadows what is to come in the 1970's, namely the Court's inability to arrive at a formula for takings law.[34] The Court at least spelled out some general criteria.[35]

Goldblatt is an important case of this period because it was the first time the Supreme Court admitted it could not come up with a formula to deal with a land use case. As will be seen in the next chapter, the Supreme Court, during the 1970's, gave up trying to establish general criteria for land use and fell into an atheoretical *ad hoc* method of dealing with land use problems. This outcome is not unexpected. The Court was committed to a utilitarian framework via Holmes's balancing tests. So, it is no wonder that it could not come up with certain and definitive results. The problem was compounded by the Court's lack of a clear understanding that balancing tests do not make for good statements of law, especially if the categories that are to be balanced lack rigor and definition. Because Holmes left a rather loose and amorphous case law for later courts to work with, they were stuck with balancing tests and were not sure exactly what was to be balanced. So it is not surprising that the Court was forced to admit that it cannot establish any set formula to deal with takings law.

In summary, whether the Supreme Court can settle disputes and provides guidance to lower courts satisfactorily is one thing, whether it can apply its own principles consistently is another matter. How can the Supreme Court expect lower courts to follow its direction, when it has difficulty interpreting and applying its own tests?

Utilitarianism, per se, is not the problem. But, utilitarianism as sketched out by Holmes was too open ended to provide any bedrock solution to land use matters. In the real world a certain level of closure is necessary if law is not to become a free floating exercise. One of the difficult problems the Supreme Court faces is the problem of interpretation. Since reasonable people can read the law in many ways, without necessarily being creative nor intending to twist it to fit their ends. It should not be presumed that people or courts are intentionally being creative in the reading of Supreme Court opinions. But the problem of interpretation is not an insurmountable one, as postmodernists would have us believe.

The philosophical dimension to the problem of interpretation is rather inconclusive. The process of interpretation is poorly understood. Can two reasonable people, look at a document, the same way? Can the implications, inferences, and understandings of texts be similarly interpreted by a plurality of people? These are difficult questions and are sure to vex philosophers for some time to come. But as far as law is concerned, being a practical activity, it is not necessary to understand the exact process of interpretation nor await for the findings of philosophers, linguists, psychologists, and other social scientists. It is said that all that an individual needs to do is comport his or her actions and behavior with the "spirit" of the law. This is not good enough. Nor is the individual comporting his or her actions and behavior to the "letter" of the law good enough. Both dimensions are rather murky. What seems to be needed is that individuals comport their activity to the "best" interpretation of the law at any given historical period. The "best" interpretation means the one that is most practical, useful, and fair. In our system, the body that is chosen to provide us with the "best" reading of the law is the Supreme Court. Whether a sitting Supreme Court in fact gives us its "best" reading of the law is another matter. This is the entity that we have to work with. If we are not satisfied that it provides us with the "best" interpretation of the law, then we are free to set up another institution that will do so. This also means that not all interpretations are equal. Although we are free to criticize the Court's tests and criteria for falling short in some way, we still need an entity like the Supreme Court to consolidate and reduce the myriad of legal interpretation.

Postmodernists may fancy that one interpretation is as valid as the next. Not so. Democratic institutions are necessary to pass laws that reflect the needs of the broader society. However, the same principles of democracy cannot be made applicable in the interpretation process. Otherwise, it would lead to confusion, chaos, and anarchy. Of course, as already said, whether the Supreme Court provides the "best" interpretation is a rather dubious proposition. And whether its interpretation is "fair" is one thing, its necessity another thing. Reductionism does not always lead to the best outcomes nor necessarily produce "fair" decisions. But it has the merit of producing final decisions. A legal system's biggest enemy is the free floating interpretation of law.

The next chapter will further elaborate land use law and lay out more precisely what happened to the story of land use takings after the dark ages. Here we will get a chance to see the Court interpreting and reinterpreting—interpretations galore as it struggles with land use problems.

CHAPTER FIVE

THE RENAISSANCE OF LAND USE

A. *1971–1980 CASE LAW*
B. *1981–1996 CASE LAW*

The body of land use takings law that developed from the 1970's to the present can only be characterized as a patchwork of muddled propositions. Because the foundation of takings law was shaky to begin with, the subsequent structure almost completely came apart with nothing holding it together other than a set of Holmsian propositions. It can be characterized as a series of concepts that can fly away at any moment. The difficulty rests with taking loose Holmsian ideas of utility and compounding them with more balancing tests that spell chaos more than anything else.

In the 1970's, the Supreme Court was awakened to a new set of land use problems that were not in the vanguard during the 1920's. In the 1920's it was still possible to blanket a community with soot in exchange for material goods. The technology was not available to scrub and filter the harmful elements that resulted from the production process. So the trade-off of more goods for a less cleaner environment may not have seemed like a bad exchange. However, this utilitarian calculus became unacceptable in the 1970's. Environmentalism changed the dynamic or paradigm of the old utilitarian calculus. It no longer became acceptable to exchange dirty air or contaminated waters for more material goods. The trick in all this was: how to solve the equation of accommodating our standard of living, under the industrial exchange model, by factoring in the environmental equation, without loss of jobs or goods? Fifty years of technological innovation allowed for cleaner air but at a higher cost of production, and this would entail a set of new norms and new set of legal controls over businesses. Of course, to calculate how much technology can be leveraged to increase our material goods without sacrificing cleaner air and water is a rather thorny question.

The Supreme Court not oblivious to these changes was forced to address land use under a new paradigm. It was not simply only environmental and ecological, but a whole host of issues arising out of the civil rights, housing, and cultural spheres. Landmarks, for example, present their own set of problems and issues in the takings dynamic. The Court faced these problems with the traditional balancing of interests, *ad hoc* rulings, and common law thinking. The Court was stuck, basically, trying to apply an old paradigm to new constructs. There is nothing wrong with applying precedent to new problems. This is the way of the law. But when there is a paradigmatic shift in conditions, then it makes sense to change the equations or model in the decisionmaking. The old industrial exchange model—the price of goods as a function of the costs of production—will not hold under these new circumstances. The Court failed to modify the utilitarian calculus to reflect these new realities.

It was not simply that its old utilitarian foundation failed to adequately address the environmental aspect of taking. The Court also continued to work within the natural law paradigm of pastoral settings, in its analysis of the social grounding of civil society. That is, the Court continued to see land use as a function of a civil society that has passed away. The civil societies of the eighteenth and nineteenth centuries had vanished long ago. Yet the Court was operating as if the civil society of pre-Industrial Revolution America corresponded to the civil society of a post-Industrial Revolution America that was beginning to enter the Information Age. Consequently, it had no other choice than to fall back on *ad hoc* solutions. Here is what happened.

A. *1971–1980 CASE LAW*

Early in the decade, the Supreme Court decided an important non-land use case. In 1972 the Court handed down *Lynch v. Household Finance Corp.*[1] The significance of the case is that it attempted to clarify the Court's position between personal rights (civil) and property rights. This is significant because the Court has treated civil rights and property rights differently since the late 1930's. The Court has been deferential over questions involving economic/property rights while at the same time increasing the level of scrutiny over cases involving civil rights. The Court, at least in theory if not in fact, stated in *Lynch* that property rights should not be viewed as inferior to or less than civil rights.

Lynch is a garnishment case. Lynch asked her employer to deposit $10 per week from her $69 weekly salary. Household Finance Corp. sued Lynch for not paying a promissory note. Household Finance, without Lynch's knowledge, garnished her bank account, under a provision of Connecticut law that allowed for pre-judgment garnishments. She challenged this law as a violation of the equal protection and due process clauses of the Constitution and sought injunctive relief under 42 U.S.C. Sect. 1983.[2]

What is interesting about this case is that the Court is unable to see why civil rights and property rights should get different levels of judicial review. Property rights are civil rights and ought to be protected as civil rights. There is an interdependence between property rights and personal rights. The Court said:

> Property does not have rights. People have rights. The right to enjoy property without unlawful deprivations, no less than the right to speak or the right to

travel, is in truth a "personal" right, whether the "property" in question be a welfare check, a home, or a savings account. In fact, a fundamental interdependence exists between the personal right to liberty and the personal right in property. Neither could have meaning without the other. That rights in property are basic civil rights has long been recognized. (*Lynch*, p. 552).[3]

Lynch won her case, but the Supreme Court will not really apply this integrated view of property and civil rights. The Court's statement here is more of a statement of ideals rather than fact.

In 1974 the Court plunged further into the civil rights and housing issues with the case of *Village of Belle Terre v. Boraas*.[4] Six students of the State University of New York at Stony Brook were living together— and none of them were related to each other by blood, adoption, or marriage. It appears the students set up some sort of commune, in Belle Terre, a small town. This shocked local residents. So, the Village of Belle Terre passed an ordinance restricting the number of people that can live together. The students brought suit for a violation of the equal protection of law under 42 U.S.C. Sect. 1983 and sought an injunction and an order declaring the ordinance unconstitutional.

The Supreme Court gave this case minimal judicial review, apparently forgetting its determination just two years before in *Lynch*. The Court yielded to the legislature to draw the line with regard to housing. The Court said:

A quiet place where yards are wide, people few, and motor vehicles restricted are legitimate guidelines in a land-use project addressed to family needs. This goal is a permissible one within *Berman v. Parke[r]*. The police power is not confined to elimination of filth, stench, and unhealthy places. It is ample to lay out zones where family values, youth values, and the blessings of quiet seclusion and clean air makes the area a sanctuary for people. (*Village of Belle Terre*, p. 9).[5]

The gist of this case is that students have civil rights but not in living together because these civil rights are balanced against the morals of the community—and the community prevailed here.[6] Whether housing can be conditioned solely on moral principles, if the aggregation of individuals does not pose a health or safety hazard to the community, is another thorny problem that has not been adequately addressed by the Supreme Court. Again, the Court is working within old paradigms rather than tackle the problem under new conditions. It seems clear that an aggregation of individuals that poses a health and safety risk to the community ought to be broken up under the traditional police power authorization. However, the conditioning and restricting of housing that force the dispersion of individuals simply because they are not related by either blood, adoption, or marriage is simply a Judeo-Christian outcome rather than a legal determination. The Court has no business restricting individuals that want to live together under a theological paradigm and rationale that has been undermined and battered from the time of Copernicus.

The major land use case of the decade came in 1978, *Penn Central Transp. Co. v. City of New York.*[7] This case continued the Holmsian approach and sets the standard for how land use cases will be evaluated. With this case, the Supreme Court jumped back into the land use arena. Unfortunately, it landed on its head—the case talks about balancing of interests, case-by-case analysis, and about its inability to develop a formula to deal comprehensively with land use issues. The Court developed an atheoretical set of tools that were difficult to apply. And States were forced to start paying attention to what the Court was saying. The Supreme Court assumed that takings law had stood still while the Court took its leave from the field. Consequently, the Court's rhetoric was more than its power of analysis—and hence it produced a humpty-dumpty sort of an opinion.

It is worthwhile to discuss this opinion in full because it has set the pace for land use takings law and other areas of property law. New York City had passed the Landmark Preservation Law. The owners of Grand Central Terminal wanted to build a 50 story building over the terminal. Grand Central, however, had been designated a landmark and changes to the structure could not be made without a permit from the city. The terminal owners filed suit claiming the landmark law was a "taking" of their property without just compensation and arbitrarily deprived them of their property without due process of law. The New York Court of Appeals rejected the owners claims and upheld the law.

The Supreme Court recognized that a landmark designation places limits on the use of property. There is no doubt Penn Central already had found a company to lease the 50 story building—a 50 year lease for $1 million during construction and $3 million annually thereafter. So it is clear that the landmark law restricted Penn Central's use of its property at substantial monetary losses to the owners.

Justice Brennan, writing for the Court, admitted the difficulty of the problem, and he, furthermore, recognized the Court was not able to establish a "set-formula." The method was case-by-case or *ad hoc.* Although the Court was unable to arrive at a "set-formula" to resolve the takings question, it nevertheless espoused a number of factors that courts must turn to in resolving takings issues. The Court worked within the Holmsian balancing test universe and made a few refinements.

The test used could be called a balancing test or, more precisely, a "multi-factor balancing test." The factors to be considered are: 1) the need to consider the *economic impact* of the regulation, 2) the interference of the regulation on *investment-backed expectations*, and 3) the *character of the governmental action*.[8]

The Court also recognized a land use restriction that is not "reasonably necessary to achieve a substantial public purpose," or has an extremely harsh impact on the owner may constitute a taking.[9] The Court, further, said it would use "whole parcel" analysis—that is, takings law does not divide the parcel into sticks and consider each stick independently of all the others.[10]

Penn Central, however, claimed they were unfairly singled out to bear a burden that rightly should be borne by the public. They had been singled out to bear a disproportionate share of the public burden. Justice Brennan agreed with them on this point. Justice Brennan said that "justice and fairness" dictated that a few property owners not bear a disproportionate share of the social burden.[11] But this is not the case here because of the notion of average reciprocity of advantage. It will be recalled that Holmes mentioned the average reciprocity of advantage test in his *Pennsylvania Coal* opinion. But Justice Brennan took it to another level. What advantage could Penn Central hope to get as a result of the regulation? The public gets the benefit of preserving a landmark. But it is not clear what distinct advantage Penn Central gets for being so designated. Penn Central was also offered valuable development transfer rights (DTR's)—meaning they could use another building nearby for their project.[12]

The Court, also, mentioned the diminution of value test. It stated that courts should consider this test, but it alone is insufficient to overturn valid regulation.

The dissent, written by Justice Rehnquist, claimed the City of New York took valuable property rights from the owners. Rehnquist said the police power should not be used in a broad sense—that it is not coterminous with government itself.[13] He believes that all reasonable return was denied, and the Court did not resolve the issue of what it meant by "whole parcel" analysis, just what portion of the property had been taken. Some of Justice Rehnquist's complaints in the dissent will find their place on the majority side in the 1980's.

Penn Central essentially confronted the issue of the role of the state forcing citizens to behave in a manner that is not in their best interest. Although citizens have a stake in the preservation of historic buildings and artifacts, the question becomes at what cost? Can the state single out certain property owners to bear the costs of regulations that are aimed at preserving historic material or due to their aesthetic value? If so, must they be compensated for restricting the use of their property? These are interesting and important questions. A brief answer is this: if the buyer knowingly purchases or should have reason to believe the sale involves or would involve a historic building or artifact or other structure that is likely to be or will be designated a landmark, then that buyer should have no recourse when the state regulates its use. However, if a buyer has no reason to believe that he or she is acquiring historic property, then the state should compensate the owner for restricting its use. Original owners of property could not know that their property will be designated a landmark at some future point. Consequently, they should be fully compensated if their property is designated a landmark. If the current owner is not the original owner of the property, then a probability calculus would need to be established. The inquiry being: what is it about this site that would mark it as having historical significance? If a buyer, for example, knows that a major war battle was fought at that site he or she is forewarned that a landmark designation is highly probable. If the owners of Penn Central were the original owners, then they should be compensated. If they acquired the property knowing its historical significance, then no compensation should be allowed.

Coming on the heals of *Penn Central*, the Court decided in 1979 *Kaiser Aetna v. United States*.[14] The case is important because it gives special attention to the right to exclude. From the bundle of rights, the right to exclude others is fundamental. Kaiser Aetna dredged and filled a shallow lagoon next to a navigable bay and the Pacific Ocean, on the island of Oahu, Hawaii but separated by a barrier beach. The pond was converted into a marina and thus connected to the bay. Kaiser Aetna increased the depth of the channel. The government claimed Kaiser Aetna changed the nature of the property. So it was no longer private because the company connected the pond to the navigable bay, making it public property. It had become public waters and the company lost the right to exclude others from using the marina.

The government wanted to convert the marina into a public aquatic park and thought it had authority to do so under the power of its navigational servitude. But Kaiser Aetna invested millions of dollars for converting and improving the property. The company prevailed. Justice Rehnquist writing for the Court said: "In this case, we hold that the "right to exclude," so universally held to be a fundamental element of the property right, falls within this category of interests that the Government cannot take without compensation."[15]

What the Supreme Court was saying is that an interference with the right to exclude can result in a taking of property because this stick, from the bundle of rights, is very important to property interests. The right to sell is not as fundamental as the right to exclude because, in the same year, the Court said so, in the non-land use case of *Andrus v. Allard*.[16] Congress passed the Eagle Protection Act that makes it unlawful to "take, possess, sell, purchase, barter, offer to sell, purchase or barter, transport, export or import" bald or golden eagles or any parts thereof. This statute did not apply to "possession or transportation" of such eagles or parts taken before passage of the statute.[17] In effect, the statute, retroactively abolished the right to sell eagle parts that one possessed before the Act.

Even though an important right was taken—the right to sell—Justice Brennan did not believe this was a taking because the regulation left other sticks in the bundle of rights untouched, such as possession and use. So according to Brennan, writing for the Court, the taking of one stick did not amount to a taking because he applied the "whole bundle" analysis the Court talked about in *Penn Central*. In simple terms, the Court is saying: The loss of one stick in the bundle of property rights—the right to sell—does not necessarily constitute a taking because there still remains the right to possess and use—even though the most profitable right was taken.

Furthermore, the Court clarified what it meant by the "investment-backed expectations" criteria it espoused in *Penn Central*—loss of future profits is too speculative for the Court to predict. Since there was no physical taking, the Court was unable to predict future profits.[18]

In 1980, the Court decided *Agins v. City of Tiburn*.[19] This case attempted to improve upon the tests used in *Penn Central*. The Agins claimed that a zoning ordinance that rezoned their property was a taking. An open space zoning ordinance was a taking of their property because it restricted the number of houses that could be built upon their five acre tract. The Agins claimed the ordinance completely destroyed the value of their property. The Court made a distinction between eminent domain condemnations proceedings and inverse condemnation, which the Agins were pursuing. Inverse condemnation is an action that is brought by private parties rather than the government, in an attempt to force the government to condemn the property and hence pay compensation. The owner is basically saying: 'You, the government, have taken my property, and I concede that you have the authority and right to do so. But, you should have done it through your power of eminent domain rather than your police power. And if you had acted properly, by condemning my property, then you would have made provisions to compensate me for my loss.'[20]

The California Supreme Court rejected the Agins claim. The State of California, with this decision, joined other States in rejecting inverse condemnation remedies. Had this not been the case, then California would have opened the floodgates to landowners that consider themselves to be overregulated to sue their regulators for damages.

Due to a procedural defect, the Supreme Court was unable to decide the main issue—whether the inverse condemnation remedy should be available here. The only issue properly before the Court was whether the mere enactment of a zoning ordinance could be a taking.[21] The Court simply answered the question by saying that the mere enactment of a zoning law can be a taking, but there is a substantial burden on the claimant to prove it. The ordinance must not "substantially advance a legitimate state interest," (citing *Nectow*) for it to be a violation of a general zoning law. Or put another way, to defeat a general zoning law, it must be found not to substantially advance a legitimate state interest.[22] A difficult burden to overcome, since this type of legislation is always coated in doing-the-public-good language. Or, the Court held, the ordinance can be defeated if it denies the property owner *all* "economically viable" use, again a difficult proposition to prove.

The phrase "economically viable use" slipped into takings language by accident, say Williams and Ernst. Justice Brennan mentioned it in a footnote in *Penn Central*, and Justice Powell elevated it to a major test in *Agins*.[23] The Court, here, found that there was a legitimate state interest in open-space zoning law because it remedies the effects of urbanization and pre-mature development of land.[24]

Further, the Court said there was a reciprocity of advantage in open-spaces: not only did the community benefit, but the Agins also benefited from avoiding the problems of over-crowding.[25] The Agins were also not denied any investment-backed expectations, because they still could develop the property but not as intensively as they would have liked.[26] This means that they could not put their property to its "best use." But, this right had not judicially been recognized. Inverse condemnation was not available here, only mandamus or declaratory relief.

Agins served as one of a series of cases where the Supreme Court could not bring itself to grant such a remedy. Obviously, such a remedy would shift considerable power to property owners. But, as will be seen, later in the 1980's, such power was given to property owners seeking damages in cases involving temporary regulatory takings.

The Supreme Court's re-entrance into the land use arena in the 1970's, after its prolonged absence from the field, the Court was simply unprepared to deal with modern land use problems. It could not even muster a coherent set of propositions for lower courts to follow. The 1980's and 1990's will prove no different from its initial jump back into the fray, as will be seen in the next section.

B. 1981–1996 CASE LAW

The 1980's would prove to be a decade where the Supreme Court realized that its tests were inadequate, and the Court plunged more deeply than ever in trying to establish a coherent takings doctrine. Under continuous criticism from theorists and jurists, the Court realized it had a mess on its hands but still remained indecisive in a number of land use cases.[27]

An early 1980's case that best exemplifies the Court's indecisiveness, in dealing with the real issues at point, is *San Diego Gas & Electric Co. v. City of San Diego.*[28] San Diego Gas & Electric bought 412 acres of land at a cost of $1,770,000, in 1967. The site was mostly zoned for industrial use or agricultural use. The city rezoned parts of the property in 1973. This had the effect of reducing the space available for industrial use, and the city also established an open-space plan. San Diego Gas & Electric sought damages in inverse condemnation as well as mandamus and declaratory relief.

The Supreme Court avoided the main issue—inverse condemnation—due to a technicality. The Court said that there was no finality of decree before reaching the Court. But the dissent caused a stir because it claimed that such a remedy should be made available. In his dissent Justice Brennan said:

> The fact that regulatory "taking" may be temporary, by virtue of the government's power to rescind or amend a regulation, does not make it any less of a constitutional "taking." Nothing in the Just Compensation Clause suggests that "takings" must be permanent and irrevocable. Nor does the temporary reversible quality of a regulatory "taking" to render compensation for the time of the "taking" any less obligatory. (*San Diego Gas & Electric*, p. 657).[29]

In fact, Brennan's dissenting opinion would become law in a few more years. Justice Brennan was saying that: from the time government passed the legislation until the point at which it rescinds it, the interval between these two periods, can constitute a taking. At the time of Brennan's dissent, the law was that if the government's regulation was invalid, then it was simply rescinded, without the need to compensate property owners for the interval period. But now if the government's regulation is wrong, then it must compensate the owners. Justice Brennan was addressing a problem known to exist for some time. That is, if a municipality lost its case, it would simply make small changes or amendments to the regulation. In this way they would force property owners to re-litigate the issue. This process would continue until the litigant gave up, either out of frustration or bankruptcy. Justice Brennan wanted to put an end to this by forcing municipalities to be extra-careful with the regulations they adopted because if they were wrong, they would have to expend tax dollars to make amends for their errors.

On the physical invasion theory, the Supreme Court, during the 1980's, re-affirmed a long tradition of protecting private property from such invasions. This is the only area of takings law where the Court has consistently protected property. And this is one area of the law where Court opinions are highly predictable. As a matter of fact, the Court strengthened its protection against such takings, by establishing *per se* rules that bypassed the cumbersome balancing test criteria. The case that so ruled was *Loretto v. Teleprompter Manhattan CATV Corp.*[30] This was a physical invasion case. Loretto refused to allow Teleprompter to place a box—the size of a breadbox—on her roof and a running wire down the side of her building. Although a nominal fee of $1.00 was to be paid, according to the law, Loretto had no right to exclude the cable company from her property. The Supreme Court found this to be a physical invasion, regardless of the minimum intrusion to her property. The Court established a special category for such takings, by stating that physical invasions are to be reviewed under *per se* rules. This meant the protection would be automatic and there would be no need to balance anything.

On the condemnation front, the 1980's were also eventful. In 1984, the Court basically demolished the "public use" provision of the takings clause. The public use provision, already battered in *Berman*, was left for dead with Justice O'Connor's opinion in *Hawaii Housing Authority v. Midkiff.*[31] The Hawaii legislature attempted to break up the land oligopoly of Hawaii by enacting the Land Reform Act of 1967. It created a land condemnation scheme whereby title was taken from the lessors (landowners) with compensation and given to the lessees (tenants). The only issue before the Court was whether this condemnation scheme comported with the "public use" requirement of the takings clause. This case is similar to the Michigan state case, *Poletown Neighborhood Council v. City of Detroit.*[32] The point in both cases was whether, under the "public use" proviso, private property could be re-distributed, with compensation, to other private parties rather than to the public. In both cases the answer was "yes."

The Hawaii legislature's stated objective was to reduce land concentration in the hands of a few people, a vestige of feudal conditions that existed on the island. The Supreme Court said: "The "public use" requirement is thus coterminous with the scope of a sovereign's police power."[33] What is "public use" is a legislative matter.[34] Only if there is a "reasonable foundation" will the Court overturn such legislation.[35] The government need not use the property itself nor take possession of it directly to meet the public use requirement. "The mere fact that property taken outright by eminent domain is transferred in the first instance to private beneficiaries does not condemn that taking as having only a private purpose. The Court long ago rejected any literal requirement that condemned property be put into use for the general public."[36] It is not the mechanism, but its purpose that must pass scrutiny,[37] and legislatures are better able to assess the public purpose than courts.[38]

The Supreme Court during mid-decade decided a number of cases that would increase the burden of property owners, by way of procedural requirements, before a regulatory action constituted a taking. In the case of *United States v. Riverside Bayview Homes, Inc.*,[39] the property owner refused to comply with certain regulations. The statute in question was the Clean Water Act. The Act, along with regulations from the Corps of Engineers, required that a landowner obtain a permit from the Corps before discharging fill material into wetlands that are next to navigable bodies of water. The owner of Riverside began to place fill material on his property without a permit. The Corps stopped him because his property was next to a navigable body of water. The Court held that simply requiring someone to obtain a permit is not the same as taking one's property.[40]

The year 1987 proved to be a spectacular year for land use. The procedural defect strategy and procrastination over temporary takings was finally broken. The Supreme Court with the addition of Justice Scalia attempted to chart a new course for land use law, by attempting to halt the expansion of regulatory government. The case of *Nolan v. California Coastal Commission* gave the Chicago School of thinking a chance to shine. The Court believed that government was too intrusive, in the case of *First English Evangelical Church v. County of Los Angeles*, and it demanded that it start making payments for its temporary interference in property. The major thrust of these opinions was that overbearing governmental interference in private property was to be curtailed. But governmental interference that had an effect of abating nuisance was sanctioned, as illustrated in the case of *Keystone Bituminous Coal Association v. DeBenedictis*. The conservatives on the Court, imbibing Chicago School political philosophy, attempted to reduce government to a minimal level. A thin government is the best government to Chicago School people. The Epsteinian theory of libertarian government seems to have took hold during this year.

First English[41] is a major land use case because it has overturned a long tradition of law that did not allow for compensation in temporary regulatory takings. This case involved a regulatory law prohibiting construction on First English's land, and this denied them all use of their property. First English tried to recover under inverse condemnation and tort and succeeded. Justice Brennan's dissent in *San Diego Gas & Electric* became the law with this case.

The county passed the ordinance because of flood problems. A flood wiped out all the building structures on Lutherglen (First English's property), and they wanted to rebuild them. The ordinance prevented them from rebuilding; the county used the police power to justify the need for this ordinance. The regulation prohibited First English from rebuilding only. This did not mean they could not use the property at all. Even so, Chief Justice Rehnquist, writing for the Court, said that: a temporary regulatory taking requires compensation; this type of taking is no different from permanent regulatory takings. First English was able to obtain compensation for the period the ordinance was in effect. So by pushing municipalities to pay for temporary takings, the Court in effect was curtailing governmental interference by forcing local government to increase taxes in order to pay for these intrusions.

The Court in *Nollan*[42] broke new ground. It overturned a long tradition of land use practice. The case put into question an understanding between municipalities and landowners. The Nollans owned a bungalow, and they wanted to convert it into a bigger house. They needed to obtain a permit to make the conversion. The California Coastal Commission would not grant the permit unless or as a condition of granting the permit the Nollan's granted permission for lateral access across their beach front property. This is known as an "exaction." There is nothing unusual about this practice. It is reasonable for municipalities to condition granting permits to remedy the effects of private development. It is a means by which the municipality shifts the burden of development to the developers. Afterall, why should the municipality be burdened by additional costs?

For example, in granting a permit to construct a multi-story apartment, the municipality may condition granting the permit upon the developer agreeing to build the streets, roads, sewer mains, and perhaps even parks related to the project or other amenities reasonably related to the project. Otherwise, the developers get a windfall. They take the profits from the development, and the municipality gets to deal with the traffic congestion, need to build more schools, parks, police, and other services. However, if the exaction is not reasonably related to the developers project, it may raise constitutional questions—the exaction being a taxation scheme that singles out the landowner/developer for special taxation.

The practice of demanding exactions was a common practice. However, *Nollan* has muddied the waters on this score, and has placed municipalities in considerable difficulty because they have to be very careful not to condition permit requests on aspects of development that are not reasonably related to the project. Furthermore, it serves as a warning that unreasonable conditions placed on developers may be struck down. So the *Nollan* decision can be very costly to municipalities if read broadly,[43] because municipalities rely on shifting some of the costs of development to the developers.

The condition/exaction provision can be found lawful if it furthers a substantial government purpose. In *Nollan*, the California Coastal Commission said that the reason it was demanding the exaction was that the new structure would block the public view of the beach and would prevent beach congestion. Justice Scalia writing for the Court did not find these reasons to be substantial. The lateral access demanded by the

Commission is not related to the land use regulation. As was stated in *Kaiser Aetna*, the right to exclude is a fundamental proposition of property law. With this case, Justice Scalia basically raised the standard of scrutiny to an intermediate level of review—*substantial* government purpose requires more than minimal judicial review, but not as high as the *compelling* government purpose standard of strict scrutiny.

Keystone[44] brought back the nuisance tests of *Mugler*. Although the Supreme Court did not overrule *Mugler*, it was understood that Justice Holmes's opinion, *Pennsylvania Coal*, did much to cut back the force of *Mugler*. The *Keystone* opinion has an almost identical fact pattern to *Pennsylvania Coal*. Although the Court reached the opposite results here from that of *Pennsylvania Coal*, it was an opinion that Justice Brandeis could have written. It sounded like an opinion that was a throwback to an earlier era. The Court in *Keystone* had the opportunity to overturn *Pennsylvania Coal*, but it did not do so because it sufficiently distinguished it from that case. And although *Keystone* came to the opposite result from *Pennsylvania Coal*, it did not replace the tests developed in that case. However, it did establish the *Mugler* analysis as viable and could be used in addition to *Pennsylvania Coal* tests. The Court apparently did not see any contradictions between the two approaches.[45]

Keystone claimed sections 4 & 5 of the Bituminous Mine Subsidence and Land Conservation Act was a taking of their property. The Supreme Court disagreed. The company was required to leave 50% of the coal in place under certain structures such as public buildings, dwelling houses, etc. This case affirmed the use of two tests: 1) does the regulation substantially advance legitimate state interests? Or 2) does the regulation deny the owner economically viable use of the land?

The Court found that the state had a substantial interest in preventing nuisance, and there remained economically viable property.[46] This case also affirmed the "whole bundle" analysis of takings as laid down in *Penn Central* and *Andrus*. That is, courts are to consider the whole rather than a single stick in the bundle of rights. In this case, the total takings amounted to less than 2% of the company's property. Courts are to measure the denominator as the total assets rather than the part. "The 27 million tons of coal do not constitute a separate segment of property for takings law purposes. Many zoning ordinances place limits on the property owner's right to make profitable use of some segments of his property."[47]

What is clear is that the Court is sending out mixed signals. Although an infusion of Chicago School philosophy gave the Court direction, the Court lacked the technical competence to solve land use problems. It seemed as if the Court was prepared to throw in the kitchen sink if it would be of help. If the reader has trouble following all these tests, don't worry—neither could the Supreme Court. There is more to come.

The late 1980's and early 1990's saw a number of important cases[48] dealing with takings jurisprudence. In 1992, the Supreme Court decided another major case—*Lucas v. South Carolina Coastal Council*.[49] Lucas bought two residential lots intending to build single-family houses. He paid $975,000 for the lots. At the time Lucas made the purchase, the lots were not subject to coastal zone building requirements.

South Carolina passed the Beachfront Management Act, which prevented Lucas from building houses on his land. Lucas claimed the regulations deprived him of all "economically viable use" of his property. The South Carolina Supreme Court, emboldened by the nuisance exception developed a few years before in *Keystone*, upheld the regulation as a necessary police power action to guard against flooding. The Supreme Court, however, said that the South Carolina Supreme Court should not have applied the nuisance exception—harmful or noxious use principle—here. *Mugler* analysis was not applicable here. The Court said this case fell into a special category of cases, where the total viable use of the property is destroyed by the regulation. In such circumstances, it is taken out of the balancing test analysis. No one knew this was a special category until the Court announced it to be so.

Although this case was taken out of the balancing analysis, as late as 1992, we find the Court still struggling to arrive at a set formula. With this case, there were now two categories of cases that bypass balancing analysis; the first is the physical invasion cases, as represented by *Loretto*, and the second is this group, whereby all "viable use" is destroyed. Both types of cases are now judged under *per se* rules.

Furthermore, Justice Scalia in *Lucas*, in a footnote, noted that courts look to each State's property laws, and by so looking, courts should be able to find out how much diminution in value each State allows before there is a taking.[50] Scalia would not answer the question of how much regulation is too much regulation here. But he noted that Lucas had a fee simple estate (whole). He also noted that South Carolina protected such fees at common law. It then became easy to see that South Carolina had violated its own laws when it allowed the taking of Lucas' property by regulation. Basically, Justice Scalia wanted to return to common law principles for the protection of private property. Also, according to Scalia, South Carolina could not apply a nuisance exception as a conclusory weapon but must supply "background principles" for its decision.[51]

It appears that although the Supreme Court's opinions are in a muddle, it has not given up the battle, as evidenced by the continuous revisiting of its tests. The Court, in 1994, decided yet another land use case—*Dolan v. City of Tigard*.[52] The case involved a factual pattern similar to *Nollan*. *Dolan* suggested that the Supreme Court was troubled as to how *Nollan* should be read and applied by lower courts.[53]

Ms. Florence Dolan was seeking to build a larger hardware store. Tigard officials conditioned the permit to increase the size of her store on her surrendering 10% of her 1.7 acre property. According to local law, some land had to remain open public space, and another portion had to be used to construct a storm drainage channel and allow for a path to accommodate pedestrians and bicyclists. She failed to get a variance (exemption) from the local authorities and then lost her case in state court. Her case was accepted for review by the Supreme Court. She claimed the city wanted to accomplish its environmental agenda at her expense. She argued that she has been singled out to bear a disproportionate share of the community's burden. The city should have increased taxes to pay for interfering with her property rather than take it through regulation.

The issue before the Supreme Court was how far may the government go in regulating for environmental, recreational, and aesthetic purposes before it must start paying for its interference with private property. The Court in *Nollan* left open the question of the degree of connection or nexus between the exaction and the impact of the proposed development. The Court in *Dolan* came up with yet another test, clarifying what it considered to be the necessary nexus. The test was called "rough proportionality." It required the city to make an individualized determination that the required dedication be related both in "nature and extent" to the impact of the development. The city need not be mathematically precise in its determination. This shifted the burden of proof from the petitioner (Dolan) to the city. Instead of requiring the petitioners to show that the law was detrimental to their interests, it now placed the burden of proof on the city to justify its actions. Usually, the State is given the presumption that the law is constitutional.

The Court labeled this new test "rough proportionality" rather "reasonable relationship," to avoid confusion with "rational basis" analysis, which is a minimal level of scrutiny. In this way the Court hoped to escape the confusion. But, changing labels is not the same thing as clarifying standards. Labeling and naming is certainly important, but what appears to be needed here is a clarification of the underlying concepts and principles. Whether this test will fair any better than the others, only time will tell.

What seems evident thus far is that the Supreme Court's rush to clear up and clean up its tests has led to an almost haphazard form of adjudication. It is sort of make it up as you go theory of law—helter-skelter style.

Clearly, the Scalia/Rehnquist wing of the Court played an important role in shaping land use law in the late 1980's and early 1990's. *First English, Nollan, Lucas,* and *Dolan* are cases grounded in Chicago School political ideology. To what extent the impact of this wing of the Court will be, with the addition of Justice Thomas, on curtailing regulatory activity, in the closing years of the twentieth century, time will tell. But what is clear, regardless of ideology, is the Supreme Court's failure to provide a coherent set of rules that lower courts can apply in their day to day dealings with property and land use matters.

The Supreme Court appears to be struggling to adequately address land use takings law. Certainly, there is a communication barrier that confronts organizations. What the Court says and what it means appear to form an unstable state of affairs. Its compounding tests tax the attention of the most determined scholars trying to understand what the Court is up to. It stands to reason that judges, with overburdened dockets and pressed for time, will not take the time to reflect on the intricacies and declarations of the Supreme Court. The most likely scenario, out there, is that lower level judges work with an incomplete understanding of the Supreme Court's intentions on land use takings law.

The next part of this work will take up the theories that set the framework for takings law. The theorists that will be discussed have bombarded the Supreme Court on just about all fronts with respect to its dealing in the land use area.

PART II

THEORIES OF TAKINGS LAW AND PROPERTY

(1) MIDDLE RANGE THEORY: LEGAL, ECONOMIC, AND POLITICAL
(2) ADVANCED THEORY: PHILOSOPHY OF PROPERTY AND TAKINGS LAW

CHAPTER SIX

LEGAL THEORIES OF LAND USE TAKINGS

A. *MICHELMAN'S APPROACH*
B. *SAX'S APPROACH*
C. *COSTONIS'S APPROACH*
D. *EPSTEIN/PAUL APPROACH*
E. *ROSE-ACKERMAN'S APPROACH*
F. *RADIN'S APPROACH*
G. *PETERSON'S APPROACH*
H. *MINDA'S APPROACH*
I. *SCALIA/REHNQUIST APPROACH*

The various tests that the Supreme Court has utilized in the past 130 years in dealing with land use takings and other types of taking cases have been reviewed. Now, the major juridical developments will be discussed, followed by a summary and analysis of various theoretical approaches to takings jurisprudence for the past 30 years.

During the late nineteenth century, the first Justice Harlan's approach to takings law was formalistic. By the term "formalism," Harlan is understood to be taking a literal reading of the text of the Constitution.[1] This approach is best represented by *Mugler v. Kansas*. A nuisance is a nuisance, regardless of costs or losses to the property owner. Then, in the early part of the twentieth century, Justice Oliver W. Holmes used a pragmatic-utilitarian approach to takings jurisprudence. With this approach, there is a balancing of interests taking place. The case that best illustrates this approach is *Pennsylvania Coal Co. v. Mahon*.

In the 1930's, President Franklin D. Roosevelt rattled the Court with his threats to increase the number of Justices that can sit on the Court as more and more of his New Deal programs were held to be unconstitutional. The New Deal ultimately expanded the number of regulators and commissions by an exponential factor that was unprecedented in the United States.[2]

The 1930's also saw the Legal Realists launch a major attack on formalism. This took the form of paying more attention to facts and data, and less to logical and legal categories. The Legal Realists did not see law as a timeless body of unchanging principles. Legal Realism holds that law is based upon political, economic, and sociological considerations, whereas formalists look primarily to law itself to provide answers to social problems. Realist theory can be nominalistic. That is, facts and data do not speak for themselves. They must be interpreted. Facts without theory are blind; theories without facts are empty.[3] There needs to be a grounding or a "foundationalism" for the building of structures—the need for the interdependence of theory and facts.

The politics of Lochnerism put the Supreme Court at the center of determining social policy. The politics of Lochnerism means the Court serving as a gateway as to what is the social good—e.g., the number of hours that bakers could work, minimum wage, work conditions, etc. Under economic due process doctrine, the Court had no qualms about checking the legislature as to whether to allow a given regulation. As far as the Court was concerned a contract is a contract. Such entanglement with social policy led to an outcry in the 1930's that left the Supreme Court reeling from outside pressure to abandon the liberty of contract approach to law.

In the 1950's the Court shifted momentum from focusing on economic/property questions to civil rights questions. Perhaps, it felt it had special competence or insight in dealing with these questions. Of course, civil rights questions ended up being as controversial (if not more so) than property questions. The Court, nevertheless, effectuated a divorce between economic/property questions and civil rights questions. The former would receive rational basis review, the later, strict scrutiny review.

Also during the 1950's, Justice Douglas's majority opinion in *Berman v. Parker* took the Court out of the "public use" business as well. What is "public use" is a legislative question, according to Justice Douglas. His opinion would come under attack by conservatives for failure to fully protect private property and curtail big government's intrusion in property matters. It was taken as an indicator that the Supreme Court was withdrawing from making policy and restaging a fight with the other branches of government. Even though the Public Use provision is in the Bill of Rights, the Supreme Court has learned to be selective in picking on particular clauses for interpretation.

There is a class of land use cases that has received special protection from the Court: physical invasions. This portion of takings, however, is very small compared with regulatory takings. The law of regulatory takings has been incoherent and muddled.[4] That is, the regulatory process and common law conflict over the limitations that can be imposed on property. This tension creates difficulties for arriving at a coherent means for settling land use disputes. And because the Federal legislature has not been forthright in dealing with the tension, the Supreme Court has been left to its own devices in filling in the gaps. Since Federal legislative leadership is missing on this matter, the Supreme Court has only been able to muster a patchwork, or perhaps, it can better be described as a jumbled set of tests and interpretations, that provide little guidance as to what lower courts should do. The Court, however, is not solely responsible for this set of affairs. The Federal government has only played an indirect role in setting land use policy. The Federal government still sees land use as a local matter. Property rights groups and the new militia are at hand to see to it that Federal government stays out of the local arena. These groups, along with other libertarian groups, already think the Federal government is too big.

The police power plays an important role in the authorization of regulatory takings. Justice Harlan was prepared to use such power regardless of how deeply it cuts into property. Justice Holmes, on the other hand, realized that unlimited use of such power could put an end to private property and attempted to balance the needs of property owners with the needs of the government. His approach cut the force of the *Mugler v. Kansas* and *Hadacheck v. Sebastion* opinions.[5] Unlimited police power regulations placed private property in jeopardy. Justice Holmes's approach placed the other side of the equation on the balance—namely, what is the cost of this regulation to the owner?[6]

Some theorists suggest that *Pennsylvania Coal* overruled *Mugler*. But this was not the case because a few years after *Pennsylvania Coal* the Court decided *Miller v. Schoene*, which based its analysis on *Mugler*, and in the 1960's *Goldblatt v. Town of Hempstead* was decided on a similar analysis. *Mugler* was displaced but never directly overruled.[7] It just fell out of favor.

Public Use questions have been left to the legislature. The Court is no longer in the business of trying to figure out whether a particular regulation is for the public use. But the Court is still prepared to review issues involving the just compensation proviso. The Court's valuations place numerous obstacles to obtaining full compensation.

Pennsylvania Coal has its adversaries as well as its supporters. This case has the tendency to spark debate. People who want to protect the right of private property—after admitting disgust with trying to apply its tests—generally cite the case for support. Environmentalists, on the other hand, attack it for curtailing the government's ability to extensively regulate adverse land uses.

Now, the specific theories that scholars developed in the past 30 years will be surveyed. There has been an attempt to include a group of thinkers that have made important contributions to takings law. A number of these scholars have been included in order to present a wide spectrum of approaches, but their work has not as of yet attained the status of classics in the field. Most of the theorists discussed here represent a wide range of political and legal philosophies, and a substantial number of them had their work incorporated into Supreme Court opinions. For example, the works of Michelman, Sax, Costonis, and Epstein can be traced in many Supreme Court opinions. The theorists that will be discussed in this chapter are: Michelman, Sax, Costonis, Epstein, Paul, Rose-Ackerman, Radin, Peterson, and Minda.

From the bench, drawing from the Chicago School of Law and Economics, the neo-conservative approach of Justices Scalia and Rehnquist also will be discussed.

Michelman's work represents the utilitarian approach. Sax's work represents the ecological-green movement. Costonis's work reflects a centrist and modeling approach to takings. Epstein and Paul represent the Chicago School of Law & Economics approach. This is a Lockean and market approach to takings—both are conservative, with Epstein also having a strong libertarian bent. Rose-Ackerman represents the progressive, policy oriented school of law and economics at Yale University. Radin represents the Hegelian left approach. Peterson's is a fairly recent model, representing the community and moral approach. Minda's approach is postmodernist. And the Scalia/Rehnquist approach is neo-conservative. Other well-qualified theorists could have found a place here. The theorists chosen represents a plurality of approaches to takings law.

A. MICHELMAN'S APPROACH

Michelman, working at Harvard Law School, came up with his model in the 1960's. The approach is utilitarian. Michelman uses a broad concept of efficiency,[8] one that maximizes total welfare or personal satisfaction. The questions of whether it is possible to maximize aggregate social welfare and whether different utilities can be compared are side stepped because he is using dollar amount comparisons rather than measuring interpersonal utility.[9] That is, Michelman believes that Kaldor-Hicks[10] efficiency can overcome the difficulties of measuring interpersonal utilities. However, he recognizes that the Kaldor-Hicks criterion is only a partial solution to measuring interpersonal utilities because an equivalent amount of dollars does not exactly measure an equivalent amount of welfare.[11]

Critics of Michelman's approach claim that it is based on a static model.[12] However, for him, utility alone cannot serve as the basis for takings law.[13] He supplements his utilitarianism with a criterion of "fairness" adopted from the work of John Rawls: justice as "fairness."[14]

The gist of Michelman's approach to takings jurisprudence is that he allows for compensation in cases where settlement costs are less than efficiency gains and demoralization costs (S<E+D).[15] Michelman's position is the most sensible in that it is utilitarianism modified by a Rawlsian theory of justice. This combination gives his theory an advantage over the others.

This model will further be examined in the economics chapter.

B. *SAX'S APPROACH*

In Sax's 1971 article,[16] he renounced the theory of takings that he developed in his 1964 article where he formulated a theory that distinguished between the government acting as an enterprise or arbitrator. If the government is acting as an enterprise, then takings should be compensated—just as any other business would be required to pay. However, if the government is acting as an arbitrator, then the takings should not be compensable. But by the early 1970's he no longer believed that this approach took account of all takings cases, especially ecological cases.[17]

In his 1971 article Sax no longer saw property as self-contained parcels of land. He contrasted traditional views of property, where all activity occurs within the owner's borders and property seen as a web of interconnected relationships.[18] He now saw property as an "interdependent network of competing uses."[19] That is, he asks us not to look at property as isolated parcels of land.[20] He developed his theory on this notion of interconnectedness and what he called "spillover" effects. He used the example of strip mining to illustrate the major thesis of his article.[21]

Government prohibited strip mining on land having a slope of 20 degrees because it exposed the lower landowner's property to erosion. Under current law, said Sax, a government regulation that took "all economical value" from an owner's land would lead to compensation.[22] Sax points out that the mineral owner demands the landowner below allow his land to be used as a receptacle for the mineral landowner's waste, and the landowner below demands that he be able to enjoy his land free of mining waste.[23] "Neither owner is merely using his own property, nor is either entitled *a priori* to have his demands met, for neither of the conflicting uses is, in some theoretical sense superior to the other."[24]

Sax's solution was to put both parties on an equal footing. Therefore, whichever use the government curtailed would not trigger compensation. That is, governmental liability would be curtailed because the government could not, *a priori*, judge which activity had superior value. This was not a redistribution mechanism according to Sax.[25] Then he asked the following question: which of the conflicting property uses was free from spillover effects? The answer to this question should lead the government to stop the party that causes spillover. In his example it was the owner that strip mines.

This view has had an influence on the Supreme Court, especially in cases involving ecological and environmental concerns. What is unique about this theory is not obvious. He appears to be saying: During the colonial period and much of the nineteenth century in America, land was plentiful and the distance between landowners effectively prevented the possibility of spillover effects. Also, technology did not contribute to spillover. With the coming of the twentieth century and problems of urbanization, spillover became a real threat, and the party that caused the spillover should be liable. What he saying is that if land is left in its natural state, the less likely to cause spillover; if land remains undeveloped, there is little threat of spillover, but if the land is developed, then there is a real possibility for spillover, and the more intensive the development, the greater the risk of spillover. So the party that causes spillover should bear the burden, by compensating the owner whose property is damaged. Usually, the party that will be doing the compensating, under Sax's theory, is the landowner-developers. That is, he is shifting the costs of development to the developers. Of course, this model works well for environmentalists and other green movement groups, but it is tilted against property owners.

Sax's model is anti-developmental, because developers would have to incur additional costs and overcome additional obstacles to developing their property. Although environmental and ecological concerns are very important, the need for people to work and build are also important factors. Environmentalism aims at high ideals, but whether a given society is prepared to arrest economic development (or the level of economic development) must be fought over in the political arena. So the outcome must be based on a political theory that is not narrowly drawn to satisfy special interests—here, environmentalists and landowner-developers.

C. COSTONIS'S APPROACH

Costonis's approach to takings is to develop a decisional model that would add a third layer between the police power and takings clause, what he calls the "accommodation power." His approach is centrist. Costonis's solution to the takings problem is "fair compensation." "[T]he concept of "fair compensation" serves as an intermediary between the police power's absence of compensation and the eminent domain's requirement of "just compensation.""[26]

Costonis's middle position is evidenced by his attack on Professor Ellickson's efficiency argument in relation to land use. Ellickson advocates the Chicago School of Law & Economics approach to dealing with land use.[27] With the exception of nuisance, under Ellickson's *laissez-faire* distribution model, all government interference or frustration of private property leads to compensation. The measure of damages would be the difference between the value of property before and after the regulation.[28]

Conversely, Costonis is just as critical of the police power enthusiasts as he is of the Chicago School people—public interest police power advocates, such as Bosselman. He is also dissatisfied with multi-factor balancing tests, as found in *Penn Central*. He takes balancing to favor more governmental interests over private interests.

> Despite the inclusion of the takings clause in the Bill of Rights, the Court, as part of its reaction to Lochnerism, has relegated property rights to second-class status by classifying measures affecting them as economic legislation entitled to a close to insuperable presumption of constitutional validity, the weak protection accorded property rights appears in the multifactor balancing test, under which the Court will decline to declare a measure a taking unless it precludes "economically viable" or "reasonable beneficial" use of land, and perhaps even in the face of such preclusion. That test, therefore, has denied property the potent network of safeguards extended to other values guaranteed by the Bill of Rights such as freedom of expression. A shift to the proposed decisional model is unlikely as long as the Court posits that the sole values comprehended by property are economic in character. (Costonis, pp. 476–477).[29]

Costonis's decisional model is formalistic. The judges ask a series of questions, and based on the responses, the judge moves to the next stage of the model. This is formalistic in the sense that the rules that govern the model are said to be value-neutral. Costonis's decisional model came under criticism from Ross.[30] Ross believes the model to be deterministic.[31] He claims that Costonis's model will fail because it attempts to replace the judge's stochastic form of decision making with a standardized and inflexible form of decision making.[32] Ross says that stochastic models assume the existence of a random variable. That is, an element of indeterminacy always exists—always making the model less than complete.[33] He believes that Costonis's deterministic model will fail because it claims to reflect the whole and accurate picture of judicial decision making, without including randomness. He further claims that such models are not suitable for resolving hard cases.[34] Nor does Ross find Costonis's model to be value-neutral.[35] Ross's view that the model is not value-neutral and leads to rigid formalism appears to be justified.

The gist of Ross's thesis is that modeling is a very difficult thing to do in law. "First, a decisional model, Costonis's or any other, is unlikely to reflect the Justices' actual decisionmaking process in the taking case[s]. Second, the concept of these types of decisional model[s] exemplify a formalistic sense of constitutional interpretation."[36] Ross is correct on these points. Nor has Costonis taken account of the problem of interpretation. It appears that Costonis's model would lead to mechanical jurisprudence without addressing the "justice" component of law. How to render to each a "fair" legal outcome without falling into particularism and nominalism? How to reach general principles of law without leaving the flood gates open for open ended interpretation—the sort of the slow death of law from a million interpretations? These are central questions of law and philosophy that cannot easily be addressed by a simple mechanical model of jurisprudence.

D. EPSTEIN/PAUL APPROACH

The Epstein/Paul approach to takings law reflects the Chicago School of Law & Economics and Lockean philosophy. Both approaches are conservative in their ideological make up, both blending conservatism with libertarianism.

Epstein has caused a stir, in the legal community, with the publication of his 1985 book—*Takings: Private Property and the Law of Eminent Domain*.[37] There are numerous debates that have been sparked by this book. He presents an eclectic approach, with a heavy dose of Lockean political philosophy. Consistent with the Chicago School, Epstein believes that current takings law is redistributional. That is, he would prefer that the police power be used minimally and only where there is market failure. Social goods, like defense, are non-exclusive. Markets are likely to fail in cases where the goods are non-exclusive because of free-rider problems. So, according to Epstein, only under such circumstances is there a place for the government. Epstein's views have a lot in common with Nozick's—*Anarchy, State, and Utopia*— where the most minimal state possible is the best state or what Nozick calls the "nightwatchman" state.

Epstein also would return to common law solutions for takings law. He would endorse an individualistic solution to takings problems. Each case should be decided on narrow common law principles. Regulatory schemes, such as zoning, are tolerated but usually not liked by Chicago School people. Chicago people do not like solutions where the state paints in broad strokes. He rejects the currently fashionable understanding of the relative nature of "causing harm." It is difficult to identify the wrongdoer in situations where there is interactivity between conflicting property uses.[38] Epstein points out that the origin of this mode of thinking is, ironically, one of their own Chicago School colleague's—namely Ronald Coase.[39] His ideas were transported to the constitutional sphere by Sax and Michelman.[40] Epstein blames them for putting Coasean theorems to bad use—to expand government and reduce private property rights.[41]

The main point of all this is that Epstein and his Chicago School colleagues believe that the common law schema is a bulwark against statist redistributional schemes. And it should not be jettisoned or replaced with statist regulatory schemes.

Epstein can usually find support from another conservative theorist of the same ideological ilk. Her name is Ellen Frankel Paul. Paul, like Epstein, finds her ideological mentor in John Locke. She believes that ownership of property is a natural right, and such a right is prior to the existence of the state. So property rights ought to be given special consideration and special protection.[42] She says we need a "post-Lockean" defense of property.[43] Paul is pushing for an anti-utilitarian approach to property rights and takings. Property rights are fundamental as far as she is concerned. "But—and this is important—pragmatic considerations of efficiency and the like cannot touch fundamental rights. That is, the right to property stands on higher moral ground than considerations of efficiency."[44]

Of course, Paul would immediately overturn the ruling in *Berman v. Parker*. She believes that this case is pernicious and an assault on property rights. The Supreme Court's deference to the legislature undercut the protection of property,[45] by interfering with private interests that were not a threat to anyone. If the intent of the legislature was to clear slum housing, then Berman's property did not fall into that category. Because Berman's property happened to be in an area that the government considered substandard, it did not give it the authority to interfere with innocent private property interests. This is clearly a difficult case, but it is not an unresolvable case nor an open ended case because modernization does not always yield perfect results. Under ideal circumstances, it should have been possible to clear the slum housing and exempt Berman's property. However, the problems of urbanization do at times require mass solutions rather than case by case solutions. And it was not as if Berman's property was taken without payment.

The Epstein/Paul approach to property and takings is problematic. The common law cannot be recovered and made to function in a way that is being undercut by technological and social change. There is a place for the common law, but it no longer can be made to function to the exclusion of regulatory approaches to modern problems. Are we supposed to role back technology to the nineteenth century in order to accommodate the common law's individualistic mode of operations?

The proposition that property is a natural right, independent of the social and economic conditions of the state, is difficult to defend. Property is a very important right to the construction of human personality and social organization. However, there is nothing metaphysical about it that requires its special protection, in any absolute manner. It is difficult to uncover any transcendental arguments that would provide absolute protection of property interests. Paul is expressing an ideological argument for preferring to see property as a natural right rather than a social construct.

Natural rights are grounded on bad metaphysics. If Paul is interested in grounding a natural right of property on Aristotelian metaphysics, she must presuppose that there exists some sort rational universe. But such a presupposition is unwarranted because not all things are rational nor predicated on a deductive logic. There do not appear to be any absolute and fixed principles across all possible worlds and certainly not in the changing and evolving day to day world that is inhabited and lived by people. The social world that we exist in is complicated by facts that are arranged not on any predetermined modality but by chance and circumstances that do not necessarily obey either the laws of a deductive logic nor an inductive one. This is not to say that we do not arrange the facts in a rational and coherent manner. There simply does not appear to be a necessity to this arrangement *a priori*. We are able to make legal generalizations and predictions across cases based on a resemblance of facts. But this legal generalization and predictability is not grounded on absolute metaphysics. It is a workable schema based on experience and trial and error. The power of our legal generalizations is grounded on a workable rationality rather than an absolute one.

Further, if Paul is interested in grounding natural rights in property on a theological version of natural law, her case is even weaker. That is, a metaphysic that is grounded on theological principles is dated because the social construction of individual identity and social organization has been undermined by modern science. Modern science has picked the meat off the theological paradigm and is starting to feast on its bones. To say that modern science has cannibalized the religious paradigm would be an understatement. Consequently, belief in an all-powerful, all-knowing, and all-caring Creator no longer can serve as the paradigm that it once did. There are people out there that will not accept the proposition that property rights are vouchsafed and ordained by God. Paul's attempt to ground takings within a natural law construct is problematic because it represents a place and time in history that has gone by. The boat has left the dock taking along Paul's fixed universe. The arrow of time cannot be circled nor moved back to a universe that Paul wants to take us to.

E. *ROSE-ACKERMAN'S APPROACH*

Rose-Ackerman's approach[46] is based on the Yale School. However, as she pointed out, this school is not as well known nor as established as the Chicago School. Rose-Ackerman takes a law and economics approach to takings law. But she distinguishes between her form of law and economics from that associated with the Chicago School. The Chicago School is conservative, market based, and favors methodological individualistic solutions to legal and social problems. Rose-Ackerman claims that the Chicago School should not corner the market on the type of economics applied to legal and social questions. She endorses a progressive form of economics and takes a policy oriented approach.

Rose-Ackernan's main concern is that the law be predictable. If that means formalism, so be it. She believes that balancing tests, used in *Pennsylvania Coal* and *Penn Central*, lack predictability. The highest virtue, according to her, is consistently following rules. The evil is *ad hoc* and case-by-case balancing tests. "Susan Rose-Ackerman is more concerned with providing consistent remedies than with what those remedies are. Formalism, which she takes to mean, consistently applied rules, is desirable, and she criticizes the Court for not providing enough of it."[47]

Predictability in takings law is essential to Rose-Ackerman's schema.[48] She claims that uncertainty creates two problems for investors: 1) they do not know if damages will be paid, and 2) if damages are not paid, investors are left with an uninsurable risk.[49] If investors are to make sound business decisions, there should exist consistent and predictable Supreme Court opinions. Otherwise, unpredictability creates an uninsurable risk to investors. According to Rose-Ackerman, efficiency has three components: 1) "private investment" factor, 2) "insurance" factor, and 3) "public investment" factor.[50]

This is what Rose-Ackerman has to say about the best action government should take when considering taking property:

> A generally accepted rule of thumb is that individuals behave in a risk-averse way when a major portion of their total wealth is threatened. Since owner-occupied housing represents a large proportion of most owners' personal wealth, government should compensate homeowners when it takes their houses either through physical confiscation or through a regulation that makes them uninhabitable. Conversely, if it confiscates their toasters or passes an ordinance making them unusable, no compensation would need to be paid on risk-spreading grounds. In short, the standard of compensation should be the individual's total wealth not just the property "affected" by the taking. (Rose-Ackerman, p. 138).[51]

Rose-Ackerman is saying something radical here. To this writer's knowledge, the Supreme Court has never espoused such a position in takings law. Even when there is talk of "whole bundle" analysis, in cases such as *Penn Central* and *Keystone*, the whole bundle is in reference to the "affected" property and not the total assets of the property owner that are unrelated to the specific property at issue. Of course, such a radical departure, in property, would require a constitutional amendment to carry it forward, since it would massively redistribute property, and it would be a form of taxation on property owners. It is difficult to see how this form of redistribution could be carried forward under present political conditions. A political and constitutional reorganization of government would be necessary in order for her proposal to see the light of day.

Another controversial position taken by Rose-Ackerman is under what conditions should the government pay compensation. According to her, landowners should be compensated when the government takes their property and uses it unaltered. But if the government takes their property and tears it down, then no compensation should be made.

This counterintuitive rule is to prevent waste, according to Fischel. If investors know that the government will take and tear down a building that they are planning to build, for example, then efficiency dictates that they do not build it in the first place because there will be no compensation. However, if investors know that the government will not tear down their building and will put it to use, then they will go ahead and build it regardless of whether it is efficient or not, since compensation will be forthcoming anyway.[52]

Susan Rose-Ackerman, in recent years, has taken Michelman to task for claiming that the Court is moving to reformalize regulatory takings. She thinks that the Court is still hopelessly caught in the web of balancing tests. She also criticizes him for advocating pragmatic balancing tests because she sees such tests as leading to unpredictable case law.[53] The biggest problems she finds in *ad hoc* balancing tests are uncertainty, inefficiency, and unpredictability.[54]

Wiseman says that Rose-Ackerman has gone too far in her claim that balancing tests lead to unpredictability. He claims that although such tests do not have the predictability of formal rules, it does not mean that they are unprincipled. "Balancing tests, while inherently less predictable that resolution of cases by application of formal rules, are not, by that token, unprincipled."[55] Wiseman's solution is not to choose either balancing or formalism but to have them both.[56] He suggests first apply formal rules to the taking problem, if that does not dispose of the problem, then apply balancing tests.[57]

This writer agrees with Rose-Ackerman that predictability is important in any legal system. And she is right to insist that laws have an element of predictability. But she carries this point too far. The other important function of a legal system is to generate "fair" outcomes. Modern civil society requires that its laws have an element of predictability, if markets are to function efficiently and economic investment not be put at risk by constantly changing the rules of the game. But should efficiency and predictability take priority over justice?

It is not clear under Rose-Ackerman's schema whether she would prioritize economic efficiency over justice.

This dilemma has preoccupied political philosophers for some time. What role should "justice" play in the legal system? Should "justice" be prioritized or privileged over utilitarian outcomes? And the foundational question, "what is justice?" It may be fair to say that Rose-Ackerman's policy prescription school of thought is not likely to go chasing after something called "justice" especially if it is of the Platonic pie in the sky sort.

F. *RADIN'S APPROACH*

Radin's approach to takings jurisprudence is influenced by Hegel's work, especially his *Philosophy of Right*. Her approach is basically left of center, in her political and legal philosophy. It is also anti-formalist. She uses the term "formalism" in a different sense than to mean value-neutral rules (Costonis) or following rules consistently (Rose-Ackerman). Radin uses the term to mean legal concepts that are unchanging and timeless.[58]

As was said, Radin approaches takings law from a Hegelian perspective. Her thesis is that personal property should receive higher judicial review than what she calls "fungible" property.[59] What she means by personal property is property that is an essential aspect of one's personality—that is identified with one's personality—one's house, automobile, pictures, wedding ring, etc. By "fungible" property she means commercial and industrial property that one is not personally attached or identified with. "Use of property as one's residence is more closely connected to personhood than use of property as a garbage dump for one's factory."[60]

Radin says that for someone to be a person, he or she needs to be able to control some external resources. "The premise underlying the personhood perspective is that to achieve proper self-development—to be a person—an individual needs some control over the resources in the external community. The necessary assurance of control take the form of property rights."[61]

The debate has been joined between Radin and Epstein. Radin claims that Epstein is a "conceptualist" because he thinks that there is only one concept of property, and she further claims that he is a formalist "because he thinks *the* concept of property can be applied formally, i.e., logically and mechanically, to yield results that should be obvious to readers and legal decisionmakers."[62] She also attacks Epstein for his literal or interpretivist reading of the Constitution.[63]

Epstein in turn picks up on the weak point of her theory—the distinction between "personal" and "fungible" property. "There is no reason to join Radin's unknown venture into 'personhood' when conventional legal and economic tools are adequate for the job."[64]

Fischel claims that Radin's idea that "personal" property should be given special consideration is similar to what economists call "consumer surplus," but he finds that her distinction between "personal" and "fungible" property difficult to defend economically. Fischel says:

> [R]adin proposes a substantive inquiry that would make it more difficult for the government to acquire or damage personal property and easier to acquire or regulate fungible property. In the former proposal, Radin has the sympathetic ear of utilitarian economists who recognize the principle of consumers' surplus, whereas the latter idea—not to compensate for fungible property seems functionally misplaced. (Fischel, p. 1593).[65]

Radin's point is not only vulnerable from an economic perspective, but also, difficult to defend from a legal perspective. According to her thesis she would overturn the decision in *Poletown Neighborhood Council v. City of Detroit* because she believes community, solidarity, and residential houses should receive higher protection than commercial and industrial property. General Motors would lose under her analysis. But how should she decide *Hawaii Housing Authority v. Midkiff*? She probably would claim that abundance of landed property, creating an oligopoly, is not personal property, regardless of how many generations the land was in the family. The problem with her thesis is that it is difficult to determine what is "personal" property and what is "fungible" property. One woman's fungible property is another woman's personal property.

It would seem that big business, industry, or large land holdings are fungible property, but what about intermediate and small businesses? At what point do we draw the line or at what level of business size or concern would she place the cutoff point? Her theory is silent on this critical issue.

Radin, furthermore, goes on to critique what she calls the "liberal triad"—possession, use, and disposition. She believes that if the right to exclude is fundamental, then why could not property that is essential to personality also be considered fundamental? The right to exclude was deemed fundamental in *Kaiser Aetna v. U.S.* And although the right to sell has not received the same kind of protection, as we saw in *Andrus v. Allard*, the neoconservatives on the Court are working to fix it. She claims that *Hodel v. Irving* is indicative of this.[66] She thinks that if these sticks can receive special protection, then why not personal property? According to her, each stick in the bundle of rights should not be considered by itself. So she would favor Justice Brennan's "whole bundle" analysis of taking. She says giving protection to each stick is "conceptual severance." That is, regulating one stick and claiming that the whole has been taken.[67]

Basically, Radin wants to move to a postliberal interpretation of constitutional property. She wants the Supreme Court to drop *per se* rules and conceptual severance analysis.[68] Even so, although the practice of conceptual severance has increased over the past decade, the central aspect of her thesis—higher scrutiny for personal property—lacks legal support. It is simply a theory. And there does not appear to be any major legal or political movement that would see it her way at this point in history.

Radin clearly is not making a meritless point, in that control over some property is essential to one's identity. And that people with little or no property ought not to be subjected to the same property rules that apply to large industrial and commercial holdings. The problem resides in its application and practicality. People that work hard for their property are not likely to be appeased because government took or regulated their "fungible" property. As far as they are concerned their identity is bound up with all their property. It is difficult to imagine many cases where they would tolerate government restrictions or taking of their property because the property is merely serving as an investment rather as central to their identity. Some people invest in a house they intend to live in. Others invest in garbage dumps. So what?

G. *PETERSON'S APPROACH*

Andrea Peterson occupies a unique position among all these theorists because she is the only one to claim to have figured out a consistent and predictable pattern to Supreme Court opinions regarding takings. Peterson believes that despite the multiplicity of definitions of property and the many tests that the Supreme Court uses and applies, she is able to discern a set of principles that govern Court opinions.[69]

Peterson was able to isolate the unit of measure the Supreme Court uses.[70] Even though this unit changes, she believes the number of definitions and applications are limited, and she explores these units and possible permutations.[71]

She takes a broad definition of property. She uses the case of *Board of Regents v. Roth*[72] to illustrate her definition.

> First, A's "property" consists of her freedom to act in ways that are economically valuable to her, regardless of whether the government has granted this freedom to A as a matter of positive law. Second, A acquires "property" when the government grants A a legal right to force B or the government to act in ways that are economically valuable to her. (Peterson, Andrea, p. 59).[73]

Based on this definition of property, Peterson believes that land uses have moral consequences, and the ordinary citizen does not necessarily accept the economist's explanation about conflicting uses.

> For example, if A wants to build a factory in a predominantly single-family area, and those who live in nearby homes object, one might argue that this shows only that desires of A and the desires of her neighbors conflict. Who is to say that A is at fault? Joseph Sax argued in "Taking and the Police Power" that neither takings cases nor nuisance law can be viewed as depending on judgments of blame or wrongdoing. According to Sax, nuisance cases simply involve two conflicting land uses, neither of them in the wrong. (Peterson, Andrea, p. 90).[74]

Peterson is basically claiming that the Coasean approach is not the ordinary view of the situation nor consistent with the ordinary perceptions of the world.[75] That is to say, in the real world real people make moral judgments as to who is at fault. They do not necessarily take utilitarian measurements. Her thesis turns on what she calls the "moral justification principle."

> The principle that no taking occurs if the government is preventing or punishing wrongdoing by A may sound similar to a "harm-benefit" test for determining whether a taking occurs. Under a "harm-benefit" test, no taking occurs if the government is preventing A from causing harm to others, but a taking does occur if the government is requiring A to benefit others. It may be useful at this point to further explicate the moral justification principle by comparing it to the harm-benefit test. As shown before, the two approaches differ, and to the extent that they differ, the moral justification approach offers a more helpful and complete insight into the Court's taking decisions. (Peterson, Andrea, p. 106).[76]

Peterson says that government preventing wrongdoing is not equivalent to government preventing harm. "To say that no taking occurs if the government is preventing A from causing harm is not the same thing as saying that no taking occurs if the government is preventing wrongdoing by A."[77]

It is difficult to know what to make of her moral principle. On the surface, it seems reasonable enough. She is right that ordinary citizens do not make strictly utilitarian calculations and are likely to be judgmental as to ascribing fault to the wrongdoer. She makes a lot of sense on this point. But because citizens make these judgments, does it make these judgments right? What is good for the individual citizen may not be good for the community as a whole. For example, the individual citizen may find it convenient to build his house in the flood planes, but it may not be good for the taxpayers to pick up the costs when the floods come and the state comes to fish him out.

The moral judgments or interests of the individual may not be equivalent to the interests of the community. But how are we to apply her moral principle in a representative democracy? It would seem courts or legislatures would assume the responsibility of reflecting the moral interests of a given community, and that they would be the final arbiter of what is moral. On the surface it makes sense to have courts or legislatures embody the morals of their community. But does this make practical sense and square with reality? It seems that legislators have their own moral problems—let alone being capable of reflecting the morals of their community, and judges are trained in what the law is rather than moral philosophy. It would seem that legislators are better off conducting cost-benefit analysis than working with Peterson's moral principle. If Peterson is interested in exploring the moral boundaries of the law, she is not likely to find it with the legislature. The cost-benefit approach has it problems, but replacing it with her "moral principle" is not the answer.

H. *MINDA'S APPROACH*

Minda's approach to takings is postmodernist. He, along with Michelman and Radin, believes that the Supreme Court is moving in a formalist direction with respect to takings law.[78] "This new type of doctrinal formalism in the law of takings has been fostered by the judicial development of a new method for analyzing regulatory taking claims, one aimed at upholding common-law prerogatives of property ownership against regulatory change."[79]

Minda, consistent with his postmodernist position, does not see the problem of predictability as problematic—whether it should be a central concern of the Supreme Court. That is, postmodernism sees indeterminacy as a virtue, and consequently, the need for predictability is not very high on the postmodernist agenda.

> If legal predictability is the key value to be maximized, then ad hoc balancing should not be the preferred legal method for determining the legitimacy of taking claims. The value of predictability, however, may lead judges to reach results that fail to take into account the particular circumstances of specific cases and thus reach unfair results. Predictability rules may lead to the opposite danger of balancing standards. In other words, arguments in favor of formalized rules merely state one side of a dialectic posed by the tension between predictability rules and flexible standards. (Minda, pp. 155–156n.11).[80]

The basic argument Minda is making is that formal rules lead to predictability but also lead to standardization and loss of flexibility for judges to take into account the particular circumstances of each case. This leads to a mechanical jurisprudence. On the other side of the dialectic, lack of predictability leads to uncertainty, which leads to *ad hoc* and nominalistic jurisprudence—in short, leads to particularism. Consequently, this brings his work into conflict with Rose-Ackerman because she prizes predictability and consistently following rules. Minda, however, believes that it is not possible to come up with scientific laws for legal problems.[81]

Further, Minda goes on to critique Epstein's work. His basic complaint is that Epstein does not realize the power of property.

> Epstein's view fails to acknowledge that coercive power is affirmed by the exercise of private property rights, and that unequal distinction of property establish unequal power advantages. Postmoderns, by advancing the case for redescribing what counts as property, offer new normative solutions for regulatory taking cases. (Minda, pp. 158–159n.32).[82]

What are the postmodern solutions to takings law? "What is different about postmoderns is their unabashed acceptance of the impossibility of solving the takings problems under an ideal set of conceptual solutions."[83] Could he at least provide a few practical solutions or some solutions under less ideal circumstances? It appears that he cannot—because he does not have any. And the solution that he proposes is more unrealistic and symbolic than the staunchest Hegelian could come up with.

> Unger and Kennedy thus argue that the history of American legal theory can be understood as a symbolic reproduction of the internal struggle of the personality. The law, like the individual, has struggled to combine the negative felt experience of alienation and isolation with the positive yearnings for connection and community. Their insights as takings doctrine seems to be trapped in a dialectic that oscillates between the two perspectives of property and community. Holmes' property-like approach to takings law may reflect the deeply rooted need of the individual to separate from others to experience true identity; whereas Brandeis' community-like perspective may respond to connection with others. (Minda, p. 148).[84]

This approach is more symbolic than substantive. There is too much psychology and intuition and not enough facts and analysis. Or put another way, there is too much psychology and not enough evidence. It is not enough to talk about symbolism, signs, and semiotics without first developing a concrete base—before attempting either to generalize or establish a system of references. However, postmoderns are opposed to establishing foundationalist systems or philosophies that rely on foundational principles.

The individual/community dialectic that Minda speaks about is not real. The individual is already in the community. The dialectic is a false dialectic because the individual is there, situated in a community. Our species exists within communities. The individual is already infused and informed by communities. To suggest or imply that property is the great divide is false. Property is a physical object, after it is stripped of its intangible manifestations, that functions under social constructs. At bottom, property reduces itself to a physical thing. Stocks, bonds, and other financial instruments are the representation of physical things.

In an of itself property is neither good or bad. It is how property functions in a given social structure that is determinative of that civil societies stratification system. The role property plays in a given system is neither fixed nor preordained. As communities change so does the function of property. Just because property function as it does in our civil society, it does not follow that their is some inherent dialectic at work between community and property. The polarity that Minda generates is a psychological polarity and not a physical one. There is no such thing as a symbolic taking of property. Property is either taken in some real sense or not. To have a symbolic taking is not much of a taking. People are not concerned that the government takes their property symbolically. They are concerned that their property is taken in some real way. The government can symbolically take their property all it wants just as long as they get to keep it.

I. *SCALIA/REHNQUIST APPROACH*

The Scalia/Rehnquist wing of the Supreme Court's[85] musing and dealing with takings jurisprudence is a return to common law principles of property law. Scalia, in particular, influenced by the work of his Chicago School colleague—Richard Epstein—is attempting to incorporate the Chicago School of Law & Economics approach in his analysis of land use takings questions.

The Supreme Court's 1987 blockbuster takings cases indicate that the Scalia/Rehnquist wing promises to hold for the foreseeable future. In particular, *Nollan v. California Coastal Commission* has generated wide interest and speculation as to the Court's future direction in takings law. Michelman and Radin have called this case an example of "entitlement chopping" and "conceptual severance," respectively.[86] Michelman claims that the Court is moving toward formalism, and that it heightened the level of scrutiny in *Nollan*—a somewhat more intensive level of judicial review than is usually given to land use cases.

Justice Scalia defended his resort to heightened scrutiny in *Nollan* with the suggestion that takings claims (as distinguished from ordinary due process and equal protection claims arising in a commercial or economic context) fall into a specially sensitive constitutional category much as do freedom of speech claims. (Michelman, pp. 1612–1213).[87]

Alexander also points out, along with Michelman, that there was a turn of direction with the 1987 blockbuster cases. He sees evidence of formalism in cases such as *First English Evang. Church v. County of Los Angeles* and *Nollan*.[88]

Fischel points out that since the 1987 blockbuster land use cases are not good utilitarian decisions, Michelman is critical of them.[89] Another view, put forward by Karlin, is that it is not simply the threat of formalism but a return to substantive due process.[90] Myers, however, says that it is not yet clear what the implication of *Nollan* really is.[91] But Myer claims that the means-ends scrutiny is a reminder of *Lochner*-era decisions. "The enhanced means-ends scrutiny suggested by the Court is reminiscent of the *Lochner*-era decisions searching for some 'neutral' justification of police power initiatives. This was the period in the Court's history (1905–37) when the common law served as a baseline for questions of constitutional legitimacy."[92] Myers also thinks that if *Nollan* is read broadly, it would "foreshadow the end of *Penn Central's* deferential approach to legislative restrictions on land use."[93]

Craig Peterson also weighs in on the *Nollan* case. He says:

An equally clear conclusion from *Irving* and *Nollan* is that the pre-1987 analytical approach of looking at the property as a whole rather than its separate elements has given way to what might be termed an 'unbundling' of property interests for purposes of applying legal criterion in takings cases. (Peterson, Craig, pp. 356–357).[94]

Further, Davis and Glickman join the chorus of the changes threatened by *Nollan*. The case created a two step approach to takings according to these authors—the unified model and the relativist model.[95] They also believe that Scalia was influenced by Richard Epstein's analysis of takings law.[96] The gist of their analysis is that the Supreme Court failed to select one model from the due process and takings clauses and consistently apply it to evaluate regulatory takings.[97]

These scholars seem to suggest that the Scalia/Rehnquist approach can be characterized as a return to common law limitations of property use. It can also be characterized as anti-balancing because the balancing test, as presented in *Penn Central*, tilts in favor of the government. So there is movement to increase *per se* rules and formalization. We have seen this in the case of *Lucas v. South Carolina Coastal Council*.

As indicated earlier, the problem with Supreme Court opinions with respect to land use is not necessarily in being utilitarian *per se*. The difficulty the Court is having is clearly stating the categories that are to be balanced in the first place. And the Court is confused over where the parameters and limitations are. The Court is in need of Federal benchmarks as a guide in applying the variety of State approaches to regulatory takings. Until Federal benchmarks are developed, the Supreme Court will continue to vacillate.

With the addition of Justice Thomas, the Scalia/Rehnquist team will hold a three man coalition in seeking to maintain a common law approach in the takings area. These three justices hold a inherent fear of government. It seems like the less government they see, the better. This basic fear of government seems to drive their decisions. Whether Scalia/Rehnquist will be able to further capitalize on their 1987 decisions will depend on adding two more justices of their ilk to the Court. The Clinton administration is not likely to add justices of the Rehnquist-Scalia-Thomas frame of mind.

In summary, all these the theorists in one way or another have bombarded the Court with criticism for its lack of coherence and mistakes in dealing with land use takings law. And that is as it should be. The Court should be exposed to the most exacting criticism that can be mustered if that would mean improvement in outcome. However, the critics, this writer included, ought to keep one thing in mind. Criticisms has its benefits, but the construction of court opinions, policy and other constructive tasks are made by fallible creatures that are susceptible to mistakes. Criticism that beats one over the head is one thing, constructive criticism is another. The role of ideology cannot be discounted, but ideology alone, should not stand in the way of a civil conversation about the legal, economic, political, and philosophic dimensions of property in civil society.

The next set of chapters will take up the economic, political, and philosophic aspects of property and the role government interference or regulation thereof.

CHAPTER SEVEN

THE ECONOMICS OF LAND USE

A. *LAND AS NATURAL RESOURCE OR COMMODITY?*
B. *THE COASEAN VIEW OF PROPERTY*
C. *PROPERTY AS ENTITLEMENT*
D. *MONOPOLIZATION OF PROPERTY*
E. *PROPERTY AND INSURANCE*
F. *EPSTEINIAN PROPERTY VALUATIONS*
G. *UTILITARIAN PROPERTY*
H. *FISCHEL'S PROPERTY APPROACH TO ZONING*

The economic dimension to land use presents a multiplicity of ideological and substantive approaches in dealing with land use problems. This chapter attempts to sketch out the economic dimensions that have challenged scholars in the field. The economics of land use emphasize parameters such as efficiency, productivity, rules of ownership, insurance, liability rules, means of exchange, and transaction costs, to name but a few.[1] These issues will be explored in this chapter. From an economics viewpoint takings law is justified only where there are high transaction costs.[2] Conversely, if transaction costs are low, then private markets should be used rather than the takings power.

A. LAND AS A NATURAL RESOURCE OR COMMODITY?

Usually, market economics favors regulations when the economic good is public and favors markets when dealing with private goods.[3] In the United States, land is taken to be a private good. However, there are pockets of opinion that suggest that the land itself should be considered neither a private good nor a commodity, because it is a natural resource; deeming land a private good is like saying that the atmosphere is a private good.

There is a school of thought that takes land not to be a commodity. Tideman argues that owning land is something special, and it is not like owning other commodities. "Claims to own land are as insupportable as claims to own human beings."[4] This view of land, in America, has its origins in the work of Henry George.[5] "Tideman argues in the tradition of Henry George. Because rights to land, as opposed to rights to one's own labor or capital, originated solely from unjustified force, land should be common property. Takings of land should not be compensable, but takings of structures (capital) should be compensable."[6]

Clearly, land is not the same thing as other commodities. If land as a whole was acquired by force, then most nations on this planet would have to plead guilty. If an individual acquired land by force, then that individual does not have title to the land. Without going into national territorial acquisitions here, land in the American system is a commodity. It is different from other commodities but a commodity nevertheless. It can be bought and sold just like any other commodity. Whether this is a good or bad thing is beyond the scope of this chapter. Consequently, a taking of land can lead to compensation just the same as it would for taking a factory.

Of course, with the rise of the environmentalist movement, the controls over the uses of land are taken seriously. It is no longer acceptable to contaminate land simply because one owns it. However, the level of control over land is a contested issue. Conservatives, generally, favor minimal land use controls and more compensation awards when land is taken. Liberals are inclined to greater use of the police power to control land use and minimal compensation awards when land is taken. But, at bottom, in the United States land is still considered a commodity.

B. THE COASEAN VIEW OF PROPERTY

A major problem of land use is determining who should bear the costs of spillover effects. It is said that land use problems are reciprocal in nature and do not have one way causation. The theoretician that has contributed most to looking at legal and social problems as reciprocal is Ronald Coase.[7] He said:

> The question is commonly thought of as one in which A inflicts harm on B and what has to be decided is: how should we restrain A? But this is wrong. We are dealing with a problem of a reciprocal nature. To avoid the harm to B would inflict harm on A. The real question that has to be decided is: Should A be allowed to harm B or should B be allowed to harm A? The problem is to avoid the more serious harm. (Coase, p. 2).[8]

The Coasean approach has served to undermine the harm prevention/benefit extraction takings test because one side is no longer morally privileged. Ironically, this Chicago School theorist's work was incorporated into constitutional analysis by Michelman and Sax, which has contributed to a utilitarian and relativist solution to takings problems rather than moral solutions. That is, the problem of takings is no longer viewed as "good" or "bad" but in pragmatic terms—who is the cheapest cost avoider?

It would seem that Coase's problem has at least two answers and possibly more. Indeed, the problem of legal and social costs is reciprocal and interactive. To answer Coase's question: Should we restrain A? If we are looking at the problem from the perspective of the "Ordinary Observer" (as Ackerman would say), then morally, socially, and politically, the answer is "restrain A." But if we are looking at the problem in purely economic terms (Ackerman would say "Scientific Policymaking"), then we should not restrain A.

Coase's basic argument is that re-arrangement of rights through the market is not free. There exist transaction costs when rights are being re-distributed in this way. So that a re-arrangement of rights should not be undertaken, if the transaction costs are greater than the benefits to be obtained from the re-arrangement itself.[9]

C. PROPERTY AS ENTITLEMENT

Basing their analysis on Coase, Calabresi and Melamed, in the 1970's, developed another frame of reference.[10] That is, they believe that liability should be assessed on the cheapest cost avoider, from an efficiency perspective.[11] Calabresi and Melamed established three rules for the protection of property: a property rule, a liability rule, and inalienability rules. "An entitlement is protected by a property rule to the extent that someone who wishes to remove the entitlement from the holder must buy it from him in a voluntary transaction in which the value of the entitlement is agreed upon by the seller."[12] If someone can destroy an entitlement, then it is protected by a liability rule. And an entitlement is inalienable if exchange is not possible. The reason for this arrangement is to avoid administrative costs to monitor and enforce the arrangement. This process shifts the costs to the party that can avoid such costs the most cheaply.[13] They basically claim that if society chooses to protect property through entitlements, then it must choose to protect those entitlements either by a property rule, a liability rule, or by an inalienability rule.[14]

The assumption is that property entitlements should not be shielded from competitive and open markets but, if there is market failure, then there is a legal need to supplement the protection of property through various property, liability, and inalienability rules.

What if markets are not open? Market manipulation is not an unheard of phenomenon. The history of the American market, for example, is replete with instances of market fraud, tampering, and fixing of prices that prompted the need for closer governmental scrutiny and regulation of market operations.

D. MONOPOLIZATION OF PROPERTY

Another difficulty involves the role of monopolies in civil society. If the government forces the breakup of a corporation, can it be considered a taking? Clearly, the forced breakup of a corporation is a taking of private property. But whether it is a justified taking is a political and economic determination. Stigler proposed the following hypothesis: "[E]very industry or occupation that has enough political power to utilize the state will seek to control entry."[15] If monopolies are bad because they illegitimately control entry via use of political favoritism, then it would not be a taking because they abused the political system. But what if it is a natural monopoly? Should the government pay compensation for its interference or regulation of natural monopolies? The simple answer is yes and no. If the government regulates a natural monopoly from the start, then no compensation should be due for its continued interference because there is no expectation of unhindered control. However, if the government steps in at mid-stream, then compensation should be forthcoming.

Peltzman picks up on Stigler's hypothesis and realizes that regulation is not a free good. He discusses Stigler's theory of the optimum size of political coalitions—of how a small group of producers can dominate a larger group of consumers.[16] Peltzman's basic assumption is that regulations involve redistributions of wealth. "I begin with the presumption that what is basically at stake in regulatory processes is a transfer of wealth."[17] His finding is that Stigler over-emphasized the dominance of concentrated groups. He found that although regulations are likely to favor concentrated groups, they cannot totally ignore diffuse groups. The political implications of Stigler's and Peltzman's economics will be discussed in the political chapter.

However, the takings power is not based on a function of the concentration or diffusion of economic power. From the perspective of takings law, land holdings or property concentration is not the problem. It is the uses or abuses of the concentration of property that is of interest to the legal system.

E. PROPERTY AND INSURANCE

Regulations impose costs. What is the best way to protect against these costs? Buy insurance. Fischel and Shapiro take up the role of insurance in the takings equation. Insurance can play a role in the unexpected takings of private property. Can property be made insurable against takings laws and regulations that devalue it? The insurance angle is this: If property is insurable, then no compensation; if property is uninsurable, then compensation. That is, compensation awards can serve as a form of insurance in cases where property is uninsurable. The point of Fischel and Shapiro's thesis is that compensation should be awarded if the parties were not first able to reduce the risk through the purchase of private insurance.[18]

Blume and Rubinfeld also take up the insurance issue. They put it this way: "compensation as a form of insurance against regulatory risks."[19] They claim that changes in regulatory policies impose costs on investors and that such regulatory changes are not free.[20] Further, they point out that the reason insurance is not available in regulatory takings is because of market failure. Hence, there is something to be said about government provided insurance.[21]

According to Blume and Rubinfeld, from an economic analysis, Sax's approach to takings is problematic. It has the same problems as the harm-benefit test. They suggest that Sax's concern over "spillover" effects can be taken care of through the Kaldor-Hicks criterion.[22]

> When should governments provide compensation? If efficiency is the sole goal, the answer is the usual one: when the benefits, measured in terms of the dollar value of reduced risk to land investors, costs of litigation and any economic costs which might arise if the availability of compensation distorts investor behavior. If there are no administrative costs, the government ought to provide compensation whenever investors would have chosen to purchase insurance in the private market. However, as administrative and economic costs rise, the role for compensation becomes more limited. (Blume & Rubinfeld, pp. 600–601).[23]

Blume and Rubinfeld would evaluate the compensation award for a takings from a projected future market rather than base it on "current" market values. They do not believe that the "current" market values are an appropriate measure of compensation awards because it undervalues property.[24] They claim the taking of land ought to be compensated based on its intended development value or as it would have been developed rather than its actual development.

What is problematic about this position is ascertaining the intentions of the developers. What one intents to build may not correspond with what one can afford to build. Having a ready, willing, and able buying is certainly indicative of the developers future plans. However, this type of inquire is susceptible to fraud.

F. EPSTEINIAN PROPERTY VALUATION

Epstein too believes that current market based compensation awards are not adequate to compensate owners whose property has been taken. Epstein asserts that the government should pay consequential damages and some litigation costs in condemnation cases.[25] He says that it is the value of property and not its costs that should determine the amount of compensation.[26] According to the law, the usual measure of compensation is market value. Yet, ironically, Epstein believes that market value undervalues property because it is based on exchange value rather than use value.[27] "Yet market process still contains a systematic bias that underestimates the use value, which is typically in excess of its exchange value."[28] The market formula denies compensation for "real but subjective values."[29] Epstein, however, suggests that there exist alternative measures of value besides market value. One such alternative is replacement costs.[30] But he has mixed feelings about this option because owners may not reveal their true subjective value if replacement costs are more than the owners' subjective value.[31]

Epstein believes the alternative suggested by Professor Ellickson is viable. Ellickson has proposed awarding a bonus value upon condemnation as a way of compensating for the loss of autonomy due to the forced exchange and to correct for market under-estimation of the property's value.[32] What Epstein seems to be saying is that markets may be good enough for the efficient distribution of property, but markets are not good enough in valuing property that has been condemned. It seems as if Epstein cheated a bit. He wants to have his cake and eat it too. This is a rather strange turn of events. The Chicago School glorification of markets does not appear to be the panacea that it is cranked up to be. If only markets would value property according to Epstein's law, then all would be well in the world.

Further, Epstein has problems with the "reasonable return" criterion.[33] He points to *Penn Central Transp. Co. v. City of New York* as being one of those cases that went afoul in the measure of damages.

> Yet today a large number of doctrines set benchmarks for compensation below market value, especially when cost or previous value is used as the benchmark. One illustration of the error is the suggestion in *Penn Central Transp. Co. v. City of New York* that the state's obligation is discharged whenever it permits the owner of private property to enjoy a "reasonable return" upon his original investment. This appeal to reasonableness is surely reasonable under some circumstances, but this is not one of them. The property owner is deprived of compensation for all or part of the appreciation in market value between the time of his original acquisition or improvement and the date of condemnation. (Epstein, p. 185).[34]

Epstein goes on to expand upon the notion of "reasonable return" in the railroad case of *Smyth v. Ames*.[35] This is a nineteenth century railroad case in which the rate structure was found to work a taking of private property. Epstein believes that regardless of the context a taking is a taking, period!

As for determining what constitutes a "reasonable return," Tarlock points to Costonis's public utility theory, as found in *Penn Central*. Tarlock says that through Costonis's public utility theory refined the balancing test—that allowed for the protection of investment-backed expectations—allowed for the distinction between developed and undeveloped property and that speculative investments are not real investments.

> If loss is based on the distinct investment-backed expectations, what must one lose? Federal law is fairly clear that a city may constitutionally deprive a landowner of the highest and best use of his property. Beyond this baseline, the line between regulation and taking is erratic. *Penn Central's* wrinkle to the "no right to highest and best use rule" is to arrest (apparently) the loss rule as a public utility based fair rate of return problem. (Tarlock, p. 33).[36]

Apparently, Epstein would not agree as to what is too speculative. As far as he is concerned government ought not to be in the business of evaluating the speculative nature of an investors portfolio. Does this make sense? The government is not that stupid. The government makes mistakes and may buy a $1000 hammer from time to time. And certainly there is room for improvement in its acquisition department. But relatively speaking the government is not going to pay for the speculative intention that an owner intends to put his or her property to or dreams about.

G. UTILITARIAN ANALYSIS OF PROPERTY

It will be recalled that Michelman presented a utilitarian approach to property and would deal with the issue of compensation through a set of propositions as to when he would grant compensation for takings. Michelman is prepared to allow for compensation in cases where settlement costs are less than efficiency gains and demoralization costs.[37] E=Efficiency gains, D=Demoralization costs, and S=Settlement costs. Michelman's propositions run something like this:

1. If D or S>E, then the regulation should be rejected.
2. If D or S<E, then accept the regulation.
3. If S<E+D, then the taking should be compensated.
4. If E>S<D, then the regulation is improper regardless of whether compensation is made.
5. If D>S, then compensation is due, correct utilitarian position.

Ackerman, also, provides a set of propositions when compensation should be made.[38] P=Process costs, U=Uncertainty costs, and D=Costs of Citizen Disaffection. His propositions run something like this:

1. If P>U+D, then compensation should be denied.
2. If P<U+D, then compensation should be granted, correct utilitarian formula.

"To put the point in terms more useful to courts, restrained utilitarian judges should be more responsive to just compensation claims as process costs decline, as uncertainty costs increase, and as the general utility of legislation is increasingly subject to reasonable doubt."[39]

It should be noted that both Michelman and Ackerman include a similar component in their propositions. Ackerman calls it disaffection costs, Michelman demoralization costs. As many others pointed out, the problem is how does economics measure this component? It is doubtful that the current level of economic development can provide an accurate measure because this category is rather amorphous. It is the reverse problem of measuring interpersonal utility, only in this case the problem becomes measuring disutility.

Chicago School people have been quick to find fault with such propositions. Epstein, for example, upon reviewing Ackerman's book, finds much to be dissatisfied with.[40] Epstein claims that the utilitarian formula (P<U+D) was not sufficient for Ackerman and that he proposed another formula to capture the Kantian view. "Compensation is to be awarded when the process costs of administering compensation P are less than the benefits B produced by the reassignment of rights minus the other costs of the project C, or P<B–C."[41]

According to Epstein, the utilitarian approach represents a "massive degeneration of property law because it treats eminent domain adjudication as an extension of politics by other means."[42]

Ellickson in the 1970's developed an alternative approach to Michelman and Ackerman. "The following modification in the general rule of host landowner liability is proposed to establish the tripartite system: a change in land use should result in liability of the host landowner only if the change is perceived as unneighborly according to contemporary community standards."[43]

Ellickson has no room for the government in this position. The gist of it is if the neighbors do not complain go ahead and build. But what if corporation wanted to build a nuclear plant next door? The next door neighbors may not complain, but people 100 miles away might. Just because the next door neighbors don't mind a little radiation, the people in the next neighborhood or community might.

H. FISCHEL'S PROPERTY APPROACH TO ZONING

Fischel, a Dartmouth economist specializing in the economics of land use and zoning, takes up Ellickson's standard as an alternative to existing land use and zoning criteria. Fischel, in his book *The Economics of Zoning Law*,[44] finds that the "police power is one of the least limitable" of state powers and that this is inconsistent with "liberal democracy."[45] From this political premise, he moves to an economic premise, which is that the police power should not be used as a means of obtaining general revenues or for reducing public expenses.[46]

Fischel provides a property approach to land use. He says that this approach has been criticized because of the high transaction costs involved in bargaining with lots of people. But he, nevertheless, believes that this problem can be remedied.[47] He thinks that large groups of people can hire representatives to bargain on their behalf.

Other critics of the property approach claim that property is a natural resource and not a commodity.[48] Fischel disputes this point, and suggests that the property approach does a better job at controlling externalities than does Pigou and the welfare economics approach.[49] He uses Pigou's example of a mill spewing out smoke. The presence of externalities suggests market failure. Pigou's solution is to tax or fine the offending party that is causing the externality.[50] And this would eliminate market failure.

Fischel believes that Pigou's and Sax's solution to the problem of "spillover" effects are not economically prudent. "Every economic activity can be argued to affect someone else. Sax is aware of this problem, but his attempts to deal with it nonetheless seems to leave no practical scope remaining for private property. The problem—one Sax shares with other distinguished commentators—is that he seems to have adopted the Pigovian sophistries...spillovers equal externalities, and externalities automatically justifies a particular state of action."[51]

Fischel, unlike some other economists, proposes a somewhat different approach to land use problems. He points out that: "public agencies will not accurately account for the private costs unless they actually have to pay them. As most economists who have done benefit-cost analysis will concede, the process is as much art as science."[52]

His solution is to adopt a variation of the harm prevention/benefit extraction test called the "normal behavior" standard. Fischel takes this standard from the work of Ellickson.[53] He takes this "normal standard" and uses it to find out what is a reasonable land use. Or what is a reasonable investment backed expectation. What is reasonable, according to this standard, cannot be either a personal judgment nor an empirical one.[54] He uses a pulp mill to illustrate his point. If a pulp mill owner wants to put up a factory, in a residential community, he should find out what the standards are for that community.

Harms and benefits are, then, seen as being either sub-normal behavior (harm) or above-normal behavior (benefit). What this means is that if the pulp owner proposes to put a mill in a community that considers such activity sub-normal, then the mill owner will have to compensate the community if he wants to place his factory there. However, if putting a pulp mill in a given community is not unusual, for that community, but nonetheless, refuses to allow him to put up his mill, then the community is asking this owner to put his property to "above-normal" use. And, in this case, the community must pay the owner. So a reasonable investment-backed expectation is one where this owner could put his factory in an industrial district without having to incur special costs. An unreasonable investment-backed expectation is one where the owner expects to put a mill in a residential area.[55] But does this harm/benefits approach pass the nuclear facility test? That is, radiation spillover cannot be confined to the borders of a community.

Let's take another example, under this harm/benefits standard, was *Lucas v. South Carolina Coastal Council* decided correctly? Did Lucas have a reasonable investment-backed expectation that he could build his houses on the property? On the one hand, since there were other houses in the vicinity, he could expect to build there as well. But what if the area is prone to flooding? Is it the community's decision to determine whether development can occur in a community that is ecologically sensitive or the government's? The point being that there are instances where a given community may be prevented from doing what is economically to their advantage if this entails that the nation as a whole would be worse off. Allowing people to put up houses is not an individual or even a community decision. There is a place for governmental input because it involves a collective good. In this instance, it could cost non-participants tax dollars to deal with flooding problems. So what does this say about Fischel's community standards? He wants to empower individuals to negotiate on such decisions that will affect them economically. But such decisions involve a collective good and the general public has an interest that it does not act as an insurance broker when a community is flooded. It seems, then, that Fischel's standard is not a complete or adequate one. It is basically a Chicago School style response. The idea of collective goods will be further discussed in the political chapter.

Several approaches to the economics of land use were presented. Clearly, ideology plays a role in economic determinations of property and land use. The next chapter will further lay out and explore the ideological and political dimensions of land use.

CHAPTER EIGHT

THE POLITICS OF LAND USE

Land use has the potential at all times to become a hotly contested issue. The players can be any number of groups or coalitions that strategically bring land use issues to a head. For example, it could be environmentalists going head to head with landowner-developers or corporations that spew out pollution. It could be government versus citizens. It could be developers versus neighbors. Or, it could be neighbor versus neighbor.[1]

The players or interest groups can either be highly organized such as environmentalists and developers. Or they can be loosely, sporadically organized around a land use issue that affects them personally, and disperse after a dispute or struggle. So there are many variations and combinations of land use agendas that can be studied by political scientists. It seems that the bulk of the work, in the land use field, is produced by lawyers and economists. Political scientists are not fully engaged in this area of specialization and study. Usually, land use, zoning, and planning come under study in the urban politics subdivision of political science.[2] Nevertheless, there is room for political scientists to play a greater role in the study and analysis of land use issues and problems. The area to which political scientists can contribute most is the study of regulatory agencies. Regulatory agencies and zoning boards play an important role in the physical mapping of communities. A study of the politics of how regulatory agencies and zoning boards influence the shape of communities and how special interests influence these agencies could profitably be pursued by political scientists.

The role of regulatory agencies on the polity with respect to property will be sketched out here. The phrase "regulatory state" is being used to indicate the sum or aggregation of regulatory agencies. Regulatory agencies, unlike private markets, redistribute and control goods and services under the aegis of the government. Free market enthusiasts believe that the private sector is best able to efficiently distribute goods and services. Sunstein disputes this.[3] Sunstein believes that the regulatory state can be an effective agent in the economic affairs of the polity. In contrast to common beliefs, Sunstein believes that there is too little rather than too much regulation.

He traces the rise of the modern regulatory state to the New Deal, which restructured the American constitutional system.

> The pre-New Deal developments were extremely timid, at least in comparison with what followed. The New Deal reformation had two principal components. The first, substantive in character, consisted of a wholesale assault on the system of common law orderings. The basis of the

assault was a conviction that that system reflected anachronistic, inefficient, and unjust principles of laissez-faire—principles that had, in the early part of the twentieth century, been treated as a part of the federal Constitution. Seeing the common law status quo as prelegal and neutral, judges (and many others) did not recognize its principles as a part of a regulatory system at all, but regarded them instead as the state of nature. Ideas of this sort underlay a number of constitutional decisions, which saw departures from common law principles as constitutionally suspect, and treated interference with market ordering as impermissible government "subsidies" to powerful or favored factors. (Sunstein, p. 19).[4]

It was pointed out in the first chapter that the size, power, and influence of the Federal government were minimal during most of the nineteenth century. The New Deal programs of the 1930's expanded regulatory controls over the economic and social life of citizens enormously. In the area of law, the common law system of regulation was too weak to accommodate the rise of the modern state. As Sunstein points out, before the New Deal, regulation was modest, but the New Deal spawned a new animal—the regulatory state. He makes the point that regulatory statutes are necessary to remedy market failure. His position is that the regulatory state has not been a failure.[5]

Sunstein also speaks about regulatory paradoxes that emerge as a consequence of regulation in his book, *After the Rights Revolution*, as he does in another separate article, "Paradoxes of the Regulatory State."[6] Examples of these paradoxes are cases where more regulation leads to underregulation; redistributive regulation harms those at the bottom of the economic ladder, etc. Sunstein, nevertheless, believes that problems of coordination and collective action can best be addressed through regulation.[7] Although Sunstein recognizes that there are defects in private markets, he also realizes that there are problems with regulatory schemes—defects in the regulatory structure of the 1930's, 1960's, and 1970's as well.[8]

Other theorists, such as Malloy, take the opposite position of Sunstein. Malloy believes that too much regulation evidences that takings jurisprudence has become too statist. He believes that Adam Smith provides the best model to remedy the growth of statist solutions in takings law.

> In particular it will be argued that takings law jurisprudence reflects a trend toward a communitarian framework while rejecting individualist philosophy. Moreover, taking law embodies a strongly emerging trend toward statist ideology which is winning out over the classical liberal conception of natural rights. (Malloy, p. 199).[9]

Malloy says that takings jurisprudence should reflect the natural rights and the classical liberal theory of economics of Adam Smith, which places a high value on "decentralized and voluntary decisionmaking."[10] He identifies three stages of takings law. The first stage he identifies as *laissez-faire* that dominated the nineteenth century.[11] The second stage he identifies with the "general rules" approach. Malloy claims that this stage is a balancing of interests between protection of private property and the needs of the community.[12] The third, and current, stage he calls the "discretionary approach." This stage is statist.

> This stage [the third stage] is dominated by highly statist ideological conceptions of the community. Legal economic convention by leading conservative, liberal, and critical voices all concur on the nonexistence of natural and inalienable rights. Rather, the rights of individuals are reconstituted as the rights of the community, thereby shifting the key referential sign of discourse away from the individual and on to the community or group. Under the discretionary approach there are no individual rights that predate the creation or existence of the state. All rights are the product of the political process. This means that as a matter of presumption the state is always free to act against the individual unless a convincing counter-challenge can be raised. (Malloy, p. 207).[13]

Malloy endorses a natural rights approach to takings law rather than a positivist (or statist) jurisprudence. Obviously, he thinks that natural rights are best protected through Adam Smith's economics. Unfortunately for Malloy's analysis, the current trend is not so clear to detect. Some members of the Supreme Court continue to see merit in natural rights thinking. It hardly could be said that the Supreme Court, in *First English*, *Nollan*, *Lucas*, and more recently *Dolan*, can be characterized as statist decisions. Further, Justice Scalia, Chief Justice Rehnquist, and Justice Thomas would be amenable to Malloy's thinking, for the most part. It could hardly be claimed that the Court has shifted to a statist position.

It is clear that a regulatory state can pose a threat to liberty—that excessive regulation or inappropriate regulation entails the curtailment of personal freedom in some respect. Americans of an earlier age took for granted the state playing a minimal or minor role in their daily affairs. A thin government, coupled with open spaces, allowed these early Americans the opportunity to pursue their goals unhindered by bureaucratic government.

Libertarians have been able to capitalize on a thin earlier American state and launch a critique of the current regulatory state by appealing to a period in American history that was short on a formal state apparatus and long on personal freedom. That is, the formal state structure was either underdeveloped or in its infancy. Consequently, by default, individuals were unhindered by the state. Whether this picture of the free individual, in pursuit of happiness, is valid or not is in need of closer examination. It is probably more theoretical than actual. But, nevertheless, libertarians have been able to latch onto this picture of maximum individual freedom, coupled with a minimalist state, to stir up Congress.

Libertarians do not seem to recognize or refuse to recognize that there has been a paradigm shift since the New Deal—not only in the sphere of politics, but law, economics, technology, and regulatory agency. Hence, the imagery of the individual staking out his or her claim in the wilderness does not fit under this new paradigm. Their call for a reversal of the direction of much of the twentieth century is a cry in the wilderness. History could not be reversed. It is not possible to turn back the clock to an America of many natives and a few Europeans staking their claim in the New World.

It is also difficult to understand the libertarian clarion call to reduce government when millions of Americans depend on government to one degree or another to make their lives easier. It is not a matter of efficiency; no one will challenge a call to make government more efficient. But these libertarians refuse to acknowledge the paradigm shift that has made the government a partner in the lives of most people—millions of Americans would not survive within the minimalist state paradigm—either due to erratic markets, environmental contamination, and the need for hundreds of other governmental activities that insure the health and safety of people.

It is also difficult to understand how libertarians would handle modern problems of coordination, leadership, internal security, and military preparedness within a minimalist state. Further, with the growth of international trade and global economic interdependence, we are in need of a strong state apparatus to look out after American interests in the global arena. Libertarians must assume that international trade can be unilaterally carried out by American companies while other nations have their state apparatus working knee deep with their companies. Therefore, the libertarian seems to be very high on dreams but short on recognizing that the twentieth century has negated their sought after utopia.

Let's move forward. So far in this section, the assumption has been that there is such a thing as a politics of regulation. James Q. Wilson, however, points out that there are political scientists that do not believe it. "The principle argumen[t] is that there *is* a politics of regulation. To citizens, such a statement will appear self-evident, even trivial; to scholars studying the subject, it is controversial."[14] In particular Marxist political scientists do not believe that there is such a politics of regulation. Marxists take the economic base to be determinative and not the state, let alone a regulatory state.

Most Marxists, for example, would disagree. To them, politics is at best a reflection of the underlying economic order. The bourgeoisie, and especially the large corporations, will acquire and use the power of the state to protect and enhance their interests. The claims that governmental authority can be used to control corporate power would strike the traditional Marxists as an absurdit[y]. Some Neo-Marxists are attempting to develop a theory of the state that allows for the possibility that political power can be assembled and used independently of economic powe[r]. (Wilson, p. 357).[15]

Further, Wilson claims that it is not simply Marxists that doubt the regulatory state can control big corporations. "But many non-Marxist scholars also doubt that the government will regulate an industry over the objections or against the interests of business."[16] Would business interests allow the state to regulate them? It is obvious that they could be regulated and are regulated in many respects. The critical question is how far will corporations allow the state to regulate them? It seems that they will tolerate regulation that is even-handed and is to their self-interest and if the regulation does not put them at a disadvantage with respect to their competitors. Otherwise, they will find means to evade the regulation.

The findings on regulatory takings and land use are mixed. Here are some examples where it is unclear that state power favors those with the most extensive property holdings. Cases such as *Mugler* and *Haddacheck* allowed for regulation that cut down these businesses and significantly reduced their value. But, as has been seen, there is a category of physical invasion cases where the slightest government intrusion resulted in compensation such as *Loretto*. In the area of condemnations, there are instances where a large corporation, for instance General Motors, had the power to displace a whole community—as in seen in the case of *Poletown*. Maybe this is what is meant by the popular belief—as goes General Motors so goes the country (in this case, perhaps, it is more apt to say so goes the community). But a counter-instance is *Midkiff*, where the State tackled the feudal oligopoly that dominated the land market in Hawaii.

Wilson also believes that the economic theory of politics as presented by George Stigler has broken down. That is, producers need to control entry, in order to control the larger group of consumers. "Not long after Professor Stigler's article appeared, political events took a turn that is not easily explained by the theory that government regulation will serve producers at the expense of consumers by restricting competition."[17] In general terms Stigler's theory appears to be a correct statement of what a monopolist would do. The problem is that the facts undermine the theory. For example, in the breakup of AT&T, the economic power of this company was insufficient to keep out competitors in the telephonic market—and not only that—its economic power was unable to stop the government from breaking it apart. So it seems that Stigler's theory is too narrowly drawn. It is not wrong to assume that producers would prefer to restrict entry and would in fact do so, given the opportunity. But whether the government or regulatory agencies allow it is an open question. First it would depend on the nature of the government in power, and second, it would depend on the pace of technological change in that particular field or sector of the economy. It is possible to have a given sector of industry maintain monopoly profits if the government looks the other way or there is little technological change in the sector. But for sectors that change rapidly, such as the computer field, it becomes much more difficult to maintain monopoly profits even if the government was predisposed to not enforcing the nation's antitrust laws.

Control of entry is not the only means by which businesses attempt to gain political power. Another theory suggests that businesses can obtain political power by capturing the regulatory agency that is supposed to regulate them in the first place—the so-called "capture theory" of regulation. This theory suggests that experts from the regulated industry are recruited to run the regulatory agency.

In a different vein, Fischel describes another example of how businesses could obtain government favor. He calls it "rent-seeking." "It typically involves convincing political or judicial authorities to grant individuals a right to receive some stream of benefits or to control some resources."[18]

The question of whether a regulatory agency can function free from special interests is a legitimate question. Pluralists would suggest that special interests are the crux of a democratic polity. Since special interests are critical components of the democratic process, pluralists would argue that special protection is not needed from such interests. Madisonian government plays off interest groups against each other in order to create the necessary balance and equilibrium that would not otherwise ensue. What pluralists seem to overlook is that not all interests are equally well financed or equally well organized. No one can dispute the proposition that in our society if a problem is serious, there will pop up an interest group to carry the agenda of the oppressed or injured. But it does not follow that it will have the economic power to make itself heard.

Although interest groups are important at one level, they can also be detrimental. Those that believe that there is no such thing as general interests are wrong because general interests serve as benchmarks of whether we are all better off as opposed to whether a particular group is better off. General interest politics also speaks to questions of equity. Whether a particular group is receiving its fair due is one matter. But it could not be known how the particular is doing if there were no goals, standards, and national expectation of what is expected from all citizens.

However, adding needless layers to the government structure without considering cheaper private alternatives can also be detrimental to a good civil society. Not only is there the problem of distribution of who gets what but excessive government can have a heavy hand in stifling creativity.

Further, is there a need to protect property interests from the democratic process? Fischel does not think so.[19] Since there is a specific textual provision in the Constitution for the protection of property, property interests should not be pushing for special protection from democratic decision making. The knot in this has to do with attempting to grant the maximum land use freedom that is consistent with others, in the community, to be free from any harmful effects to themselves and the environment, and with the minimum need to add to the current level of bureaucracy.

Some, or perhaps a majority, would argue that large bureaucracies are the problem. Rather than viewing bureaucracies as problem solvers, they are usually viewed as the problem. There are extremists, such as the new militia groups, property rights groups, and libertarian in general that view bureaucracy as the enemy of the people. They base their faith in markets and the common law to set matters right.

In the land use context, for example, there are fringe opinions that suggest that the best protection to private property is the ability to buy exemptions from regulation, and in this way not only is property protected, but it also cuts back the interventionist state. This view suggests that courts "abandon their opposition to the sale of regulatory exemption and reconceive the state's police power as an alienable servitude."[20] This is a radical reconceptualization of takings law. Its gist is the sale of state powers to those who have the money "to escape regulation."[21] This position is the worst of all worlds. It could lead to Social Darwinism, if it the state wore up for sale to the highest bidder.

After all is said and done, is it politically possible to endorse a regulatory state that exists independent of the common law traditions that shaped the contours and laid out the legal parameters of the United States? This is a tall question, and it is a difficult one to answer. There are theorists that believe that it is not possible. Friedman, for example, argues that: "For one thing, regulation is not and cannot be independent of the Bill of Rights, the Fourteenth Amendment, American federalism, or even the common law tradition."[22]

Friedman believes that, in order to understand the limits of regulation, it has to be placed in the context of American legal culture.[23] That is, the new regulatory state may have breached the common law tradition, and furthermore, the regulatory state may be incompatible with the common law tradition. Nevertheless, even if the current regulatory state is incompatible with such a tradition, it is necessary to move forward and not backwards. Though there is much to learn from the past, the past is a closed book. Traditions are important, but traditions cannot survive with the accelerated pace of technological change. Traditions survive best in static economies with very little technical innovation. We live in a period in history of fast paced technical change and rapid economic turnover and activity. And also since the New Deal, America has undergone political innovation. There is no turning back to the agrarian America of the past.

Early twentieth century America underwent a political experiment—the New Deal—that transformed the common law tradition. Did it eliminate the common law? It did not. It did however cut back its influence. The traditional view that linked property with liberty was also broken. Reich,[24] writing in the early 1960's, said:

> During the industrial revolution, when property was liberated from feudal restraints, philosophers hailed property as the basis of liberty, and argued that it must be free from the demands of government or society. But as private property grew, so did abuses resulting from its use. In a crowded world, a man's use of his property increasingly affected his neighbor, and one man's exercise of a right might seriously impair the rights of others. (Reich, p. 772).[25]

Essentially, Reich argued that early twentieth century American reformers saw property as a threat to liberty rather than its ally, and they pushed to effectuate a separation.[26]

> During the first half of the twentieth century the reformers enacted into law their conviction that private property was a chief enemy of society and of individual liberty. Property was subjected to "reasonable" limitations in the interest of society. The regulatory agencies, federal and state, were born of the reform. In sustaining these major inroads on private property, the Supreme Court rejected the older idea that property and liberty were one, and wrote a serious of classic opinions upholding the power of the people to regulate and limit private rights. (Reich, p. 773).[27]

Reich is correct in that the Supreme Court did effectuate such a separation in the late 1930's. But, again, the degree of displacement of the common law, is difficult to ascertain. In property law, land use controls and zoning exist side by side with the common law and not instead of or despite of. If its displacement can be felt, it would be the wider scope and influence that are cut by statutory controls. But neo-positive law theorists that favor wider use of regulation and less common law are not free from their natural law critics that see property as a natural right that exists prior to the state and as a bulwark of freedom.[28]

To have rights prior to community is an oxymoron. Individuals do not exist onto themselves and it is difficulty understanding why they would have rights predating their community. We are social beings by nature and we have those rights and responsibilities that flow out of our association with others. It seems that the natural law theorists have the cart before the horse.

In summary, the regulatory state breaks with early American tradition. This work does not present the regulatory state as a metaphysical entity. The modern regulatory state should be seen as an integral component of day to day life rather than as some abstract entity that superimposes its will on citizens. This work has attempted to present the regulatory state as an aggregate rather than as a body that has fallen from the heavens. Its unity is derived from the coordination of parts rather than by a singular entity. The sum of the parts holds some real power rather than being a figment of the imagination. The modern state as presented here does not subsume private markets or private initiative or activity. However, it does attempt to coordinate atomistic private activity and re-direct private energies under different principles than the logic of the market.

The paradigm shift that has ushered in the current regulatory state structure has made thin government the exception rather than the rule of the modern polity. However, modern citizens have not fully come to terms with the regulatory state structure. In popular circles the regulatory state is usually seen as an unhealthy appendage or as an undesirable consequence of market failure or as an usurpation of power by greedy bureaucrats or just an unnecessary expense for citizens that do not need government to tell them how to spend their money.

Clearly, the regulatory state structure imposes costs and obligations that could be eliminated with a minimalist state or thin government. But in light of existing alternatives, it would be wrong to grant citizens more freedom than they need. Our species does not do well when left to its own devices. Our species is an extremely dangerous one. It is not necessary to measure the rivers of blood that has been needlessly spilled throughout our so called civilized history. The state is not a panacea or cure all, but the best means at our disposal to prevent citizens from being at each others throats. And as long as our species remains a social animal, it will continue to group and structure itself into a state pattern or formation. However, this work does not want to replace one metaphysical entity, or Deity, with a metaphysical regulatory state of sorts. There is a need for a regulatory state that is down in the trenches rather than pie in the sky.

In the next chapter, the philosophic import of property and land use issues will be reviewed.

CHAPTER NINE

PHILOSOPHY OF PROPERTY AND TAKINGS LAW

Takings jurisprudence is a function of a general theory of property. The general philosophy of property is beyond the scope of this chapter. However, takings law will be placed in a wider context, in order to better understand its role in civil society. John Locke receives more than his share of references in current takings jurisprudence. Whether his labor theory of value is a good foundation to rest takings philosophy is hotly debated and contested. There are other philosophers that provide a general framework for property—Aristotle, Augustine, Aquinas, Social Contract philosophers, Hume, Kant, Hegel, and Marx to mention only but a few. Two will receive special consideration here: Locke and Hegel.

Michelman, in his 1967 paper, reviewed in general terms, a number of philosophers that made a contribution to the philosophy of property.[1] He refers to John Locke's theory of property as a "desert theory." According to Locke, the basis for the acquisition of property is the amount of labor expended on the raw material of nature. A mixing of one's labor with the raw resources of nature gives one the right to appropriate the stuff of nature or nature's bounty. It has been pointed out by Michelman that this position is hard to defend.[2]

Basing property acquisition solely on a labor theory is problematic. On a broader level, post-industrial society puts into question the whole notion of work as it is applied under modern circumstances. The concept of labor itself is continuously undergoing changes as technological innovation warrants. The variations of labor differ. So that there are no longer two separate types of labor: manual labor and intellectual labor. It is no longer an either or proposition. Consequently, one cannot easily apply the Lockean notion to modern circumstance.

Technology has undermined the traditional concept of labor, or supplanted it, by transforming the concept of work. The physical manipulation of nature is increasingly coming from the accumulation of data rather than from brute force. Also, the utilization of information and data is increasingly being manipulated and processed by computers rather than brain cells. For example, digital systems are more efficient in crunching numbers than humans. The information age is displacing not simply the use of muscle power with machine power but also substituting brain power with digital power. That is, the increasing role of computers doing work that previously required low level intellectual activity. As computers become more powerful, they will continue to erode work that is done by middle and upper management. The point being that the nature of work is being transformed, and there is a need to re-conceptualized the traditional understanding of work. Hence, the

Lockean conceptualization of work is being undermined in the information age.

Hegel, on the other hand, is taken to be the representative of the personality theories of property.[3] It is difficult to fully understand what this personality theory of property entails. On the intuitive level, it seems straight forward enough. We need property to survive, and our possessions matter to us, or perhaps most of us. And perhaps to some degree we are an extension of our possessions, or put better, our possessions are an extension of us. It is reasonable to assume that to what degree they contribute to one's personality would depend on the preferences of each individual. And, perhaps, we can even come up with a general statement of jurisprudence that the State has no business interfering in that property that is most essential to our existence. Property that is essential to personal survival should be free from State intervention. But this mode of thinking is too open ended because each individual will designate different types of property as personally essential.

A couple of examples of theories that are based on personality are Reich's theory of property in which "property functions to nourish and protect personality."[4] Radin's theory of property also privileges personality in the ownership of property. Michelman does not find merit in these theories. But, nevertheless, they may still have a limited use. A recognition that an individual needs to control some natural resources to survive and develop does not appear to be a meritless point. Morris Cohen, also, finds such personality theories rather vague.[5] Cohen sees such theories as attempts to "deduce the right of property from the individual's right to act as a free personality."[6]

Liberals have an affinity for Hegel's rendition of property. Conservatives have a similar affinity for Locke's labor theory of property. Epstein stresses possession as the root of title or ownership. He asks, how does one acquire ownership of un-owned things?[7] Epstein's response is to take possession of them. He believes that Locke's labor theory aids his possessory theory of ownership.[8] But he departs from Locke with respect to Locke's proviso that enough natural resources be left over for others.

> Thus in his articulation of the famous Lockean proviso, he [Locke] insists that individual appropriation does not constitute a violation of the rights of others, at least where there is "enough and as good left in common for others." Yet to make this condition is to undercut utterly the strong individualistic element in the rule of first possession, as the provision if logically applied makes it impossible for anyone *ever* to acquire ownership of anything so long as there are conditions of scarcity. (Epstein, p. 1228).[9]

Tideman takes something of a different approach. He reads Locke as saying that it is a mixture of labor with resources. "[T]he use of these resources is proper provided that resources of the same value are left over for others."[10]

Tideman takes this Lockean distinction and claims that the Supreme Court recognizes that claims over the land itself and claims over the resources of the land are not one and the same, and that the Supreme Court is prepared to treat the two differently, with respect to the idea of investment-backed expectations.

> Indirect evidence of the Supreme Court's recognition that land and natural resources requires different treatment than other assets, in takings cases is provided by the rule that the frustration of "reasonable investment-backed expectations" is a taking that requires compensation. While this rule is too new for us to be completely confident how it will be applied, it is noteworthy that the economic definition of investment is not "the purchase of an asset that is expected to yield its owner a return," but rather "an increase in the stock of capital (provided goods that are used to produce other goods)." Thus land and natural resources are not components of capital. From an economic perspective, the purchase of land or natural resources does not qualify as investment. (Tideman, p. 1725–1726).[11]

The Supreme Court is prepared to treat land differently from capital goods. Land, capital, and labor are factors of production and, hence, each is a component of the production process. But Tideman does not stop here. He essentially claims that the land component is not private property.

> The idea that land and natural resources are common property has been a hidden influence on recent takings decisions. Courts will be unable to employ this idea openly until it gains widespread public acceptance, for any unpopular rule that courts sought to impose would be seen as inconsistent with our tradition of popular government and would be overturned by democratic process. (Tideman, pp. 1728–1729).[12]

Clearly, Tideman is saying something radical. Frankly, this writer does not see such a trend nor could Tideman's reading of Supreme Court opinions be confirmed. Whatever is the basis of his claim must rest with his own reasoning and not by the facts. He is correct to the extent that such a distinction could not be applied by the courts either openly or otherwise because it is a radical departure from common practice. The implementation of such a rule would require that it be first fought over in the political arena. Takings law, today, does not make the distinction that Tideman makes between land and natural resources from capital goods. Private property is private property. And even if there are procedural differences in handling the two types of property, the bottom line is that they are both taken to be private.

At a deeper philosophical level, what constitutes "ownership" is a debatable issue. A.M. Honore, in the tradition of Hohfeld, Cohen, and other writers, elaborates on the components that make up property. He lists eleven incidents of ownership, but Honore believes, like other writers since Hohfeld, that at the semantic level, the term "ownership" should not be applied to things. Ownership is in reference to the owner and not the thing owned. That is, the term "ownership" connotes a relationship of rights and not possession of things. Honore seems to break new ground in not conceiving "ownership" as solely a relationship of competing rights. Where Honore differentiates himself from writers like Hohfeld and Cohen is the realization that property rights between owners alone is not enough to explain the concept of "ownership."

> Of course, the force of the proposal is a protection against the habit of thinking of the ownership of a thing, particularly a material object, as if it consisted only in a relation between a person and a thing, and not at all in relation between the owner and other persons. Yet to speak always of owning rights rather than things would be doubly misleading. Ownership, as we have seen, is not just a bundle of rights, as it is no help toward understanding our society to speak as if it were. Secondly, the idiom which directly couples the owner with the thing owned is far from pointless; where the right to exclude others exists, there is indeed (legally) a very special relation between the holder of the right and the thing, and this is a relational way of marking it. (Honore, p. 134).[13]

Honore is making a very important point. He recognizes that property should be seen as a relation between owners rather than between owners and things. But he recognizes that "things" cannot drop out or disappear from this relation because it is the objects that give rise and meaning to the relation in the first place. Honore seems implicitly to be saying that scholars that simply consider property as a relation between owners are missing the material component and the force of property ownership in the social world. That is, to exclude the "thing" is problematic because one's relation to things determines one's power in the material world.

This mistake is being made by scholars of more recent vintage. For example, Grunebaum says: "The word 'property' is banished from these pages and left to the metaphysicians for several reasons."[14] He goes on to explain:

> [T]he word 'property' seems to connote something in the thing or object rather than the idea that ownership is a relation between persons with respect to things. Ownership is a set of relations constituted by rights and duties

> among persons. There is nothing in the object owned which marks it off as mine, yours, or ours. Second, the word 'property' is too often used to refer to land or what is called real property. 'Ownership' has a much broader connotation. (Grunebaum, pp. 3–4).[15]

Grunebaum is correct to the extent that property is a relation between owners. His definition, however, excludes the "thing" from the relation, and yet it is the thing that is determinative of the relation. There is no need to leave the word "property" to the metaphysicians. It connotes things because things are the basis of ownership—to have ownership and not consider things—is to have an empty concept.

What is clear is that naming and re-naming can have a role in eliminating ghost problems that had occupied earlier generations of philosophers. However, if this process is carried too far, it can lead to the elimination of real problems because their solution is not easily obtainable. If all philosophic problems lend themselves to easy answers, then we could dispense with philosophers at once. Property and valuation problems are not of the sort that lend themselves to easy answers. One major complaint is that there never seems to be closure or completion to philosophic problems. This is a simplistic view. Each generation of philosophers does not find the same exact property problem as the previous generation. Consequently, each generation is attempting to provide a better understanding to a problem that resembles the problem of the past but is not an exact duplicate of that problem.

However, some modern philosophers have shown a readiness to ditch traditional philosophic problems precisely on this point. For example, the correspondence theory of truth is one area that many modern philosophers have attempted to eliminate because of its difficulty. However, this problem cannot easily be avoided because it has real world consequences. The postmodern philosophic attack on the "correspondence" theory of truth spills over to legal analysis.[16] That is, if one no longer connects ideas to facts/things as representing a true state of affairs, then one must rely on relations that are internal or context bound to determine the correct state of affairs. By analogy, a relation between owners that neglects the nature of the property in question is empty. That is, a relation that lacks an object cannot be a true relation. Clearly, the linguistic turn of things makes talking about correspondence problematic. But for purposes of legal analysis, a practical and workable concept of the correspondence theory of truth is a necessity, even though it may lack a coherent metaphysical crispness. It is a violation of common sense to eliminate a representational world because we lack a perfect linguistic understanding of how ideas (thoughts, concepts, conceptions, words, phrases, labels, etc.) correspond to things.

Although modern philosophers have gone about eliminating traditional problems by re-subscribing them in texts, Locke and Hegel at least sought to explain property valuations rather than resort to the philosophy of elimination. By textualizing real world problems, it becomes easy to eliminate them by dismissal. The modern realization appears to be that those who have the power to name have the power to control. We bring objects into the world by naming them, and we remove objects by voiding their names. If an object has no name, then it does not exist; something like if you don't see it, it is not there.

It is one thing to discover that problems that once seemed real have turned out to be illusory. But it is another matter if this process is carried too far. When we have a series of interpretations and no particular interpretation is privileged, then this process throws overboard the need for experts. The text remains open to limitless readings and no single reading is privileged. This is the ultimate democratization of knowledge, by dissolving the privileged reader. Whether reading texts and acquisition of knowledge is one and the same thing is a rather dubious proposition. It is safe to assume that there is more to acquiring knowledge than reading texts. Reading texts is one means to knowledge but certainly not the exclusive means.

An earlier generation of positivists made a mistake in thinking that if a problem did not lend itself to exact scientific solutions, it should be thrown overboard, dismissed, or labeled a ghost problem. It is hoped that a new generation of positivists have learned that not all problems lend themselves to scientific resolution and yet deserve attention. Even the natural sciences did not measure up to the exactitude demanded by the earlier generation of positivists.

The problem of valuations, for example, is one of those problems that at face value may seem illusory, since it does not lend itself to easy answers. For the market economist, X has value because Y is willing to pay Z dollars for it. That is it, the end. But where the problem ends for the economist, it begins for the philosopher. Market value is a subset of the notion or idea of value. How to examine this broader notion of value without falling into subjectivism or psychologism is an important matter that should not be dismissed as illusory because it has applications in the real world. For example, the legal system is in need of a broader understanding of "value" because market value does not always provide for "just" or "fair" outcomes.

The important point to keep in mind, when looking at the philosophy of property, is not to re-subscribe property problems in texts or empty legal relations that exclude the real world understanding of property—which is an important organizing force in the lives of people. Property matters to people not simply because it is a financial asset but a self-sustaining material objet. Hopefully, a new generation of neo-positivists and neo-behaviorists would be able to shed new light on old problems. Eliminating philosophical ghosts where necessary, but always keeping their feet on the ground.

CONCLUSION

It is clear that doctrines change and Supreme Court justices come and go. Some doctrines enjoy longevity and others are swept away, or worse, ignored entirely. The takings clause, regarding land use, has waxed and waned in its influence. Under the first Justice Harlan's interpretation of the Constitution to "take" is read literally, and the police power is properly used to stop nuisances irrespective of the costs in doing so. This is a formal reading of the Constitution. It is exemplified with the case of *Mugler v. Kansas*.

Justice Holmes, writing for the Court in the early 1920's, read the Constitution differently. His approach was utilitarian-pragmatic. The best example of this approach is *Pennsylvania Coal Co. v. Mahon*. Justice Holmes, working through balancing tests, established a set of criteria that continue unabated until this day. The problems encountered in dealing with balancing tests are that they are atheoretical, lack predictability, and difficult to establish general rules of application. The balancing test in *Pennsylvania Coal* is tilted in favor of private property owners. The criteria Holmes used there are not only difficult to apply but open ended, since he failed to specify where along the continuum a regulation became a taking.

The criteria in *Pennsylvania Coal* were refined in *Penn Central Transp. Co. v. City of New York*. However, the balancing test in *Penn Central* is tilted in the government's favor. So, although balancing interests remains the standard, different Courts, applying the test, can tilt it in either direction.

Although the Supreme Court has been consistent in its application of rules involving physical takings, it has not been able to develop a set formula in dealing with regulatory takings. Consequently, its decisions and tests are sort of free floating. Unpredictability and multiplicity of tests have led many theorists to conclude that there is a need for the Court to continuously re-visit this important area of the law on a regular basis, since it thrust itself onto the land use landscape in the 1970's, until it gets it right. And theorists have not let up with the bombardment of criticism since the Court jumped back into the fray.

The Supreme Court in recent years appears to be moving toward formalism, in establishing rules to handle regulatory takings. That is, it is relying on *per se* rules rather than balancing to achieve greater stability and predictability of its case law. This has been seen in cases like *Loretto v. Teleprompter Manhattan CATV Corp.* and *Lucas v. South Carolina Coastal Council*. However, balancing tests still remain the dominant means of analyzing takings cases.

In dealing with takings law, the Court has a steady grip on the compensation question involving land use and other takings cases, and continues to be the ultimate arbiter on such questions. However, it has relegated "public use" questions to the legislature. This has been seen in cases such as *Berman v. Parker* and *Hawaii Housing Authority v. Midkiff* and, at the state level, *Poletown Neighborhood Council v. City of Detroit*.

Although the Supreme Court since the 1930's has not provided full judicial review in matters involving property/economic questions, it is a mistake to believe the popular view or common understanding that it no longer is effectively checking the legislature. This work has shown that this is an over-simplified view. Cases such as *First English Evangelical Church v. County of Los Angeles, Nollan v. California Coastal Commission, Lucas v. South Carolina Coastal Council* and *Dolan v. City of Tigard* show that the Supreme Court is curtailing the level of interference that municipalities are allowed, with respect to private property.

As repeatedly stated in this work, the police power has always been limited to one degree or another. So the Court, even under Justice Harlan's generous reading of the police power, has not allowed police power regulations to reduce property value to zero. The history of reading the police power is a history of the Court putting limits on its use. When cases such as *Mugler v. Kansas* or *Hadacheck v. Sebastion* were read broadly by legislatures, *Pennsylvania Coal Co. v. Mahon* emerged to counterpoise that reading of the Constitution.

Each of the theorists has contributed a body of work that can serve to provide for a wide perspective of the different approaches to the analysis of takings jurisprudence. If these theorists are read closely, each deals with how the Supreme Court should ultimately redistribute private property. If each of these theorists is read in a broader context, they show a struggle taking place as to where power lies and who has the authority to redistribute property.

Whether the theorist is left of center or right of center, whether he or she relies on markets or government agencies to distribute property, the bottom line is who has the power and authority to effectuate redistributions of property? Of course, the conservative theorists rely on markets, and liberal theorists are more readily amenable to the use of regulatory agencies—both are likely to turn to government when goods are considered "public" or where there is market failure.

Theorists that emphasize efficiency and predictability, such as Rose-Ackerman were discussed. She values consistently following rules and would welcome more *per se* rules in dealing with land use issues rather than deal with messy balancing tests. If this means formalism, then so be it.

The Chicago School of Law & Economics has consistently opposed massive government intervention in the land use area. Although Coase started out as a Chicago School theorist, his work was imported into constitutional analysis by theorists such as Michelman and Sax. They have emphasized the relativist nature of legal and social problems—that social interaction entails multiple causal factors and placing blame on the most obvious element may not make good economic sense. They also used Coase's work to explain the need for greater government intervention in private property concerns, beyond what Coase would personally endorse. Other theorists that currently embody the Chicago School approach are Epstein and Paul. They usually ground their theories in natural rights language and use the philosophy of John Locke as their guide.

Radin takes a left of center approach and relies on the philosophy of Hegel as her guide. Radin would use two levels of judicial review, based on whether the property is "personal" or "fungible."

Peterson thinks that the moral justification principle best accounts for everyday perceptions and judgments on land use takings rather than the Coasean approach. She would use moral principles to judge the incompatibility of land uses.

Minda's postmodernist approach sees no problem with questions of predictability. He takes indeterminacy to be a virtue in land use matters. Of course, people in the real world that base important decisions and investments on Supreme Court opinions may take issue with Minda.

Scalia/Rehnquist present a common law view of takings. The cases of *Nollan* and *Lucas* represent their approach. *Nollan* heightened the level of scrutiny that is usually given to property cases. They derive their approach from the Chicago School for the most part.

Market economists such as Fischel favor a property right approach. They usually counterpoise their view with welfare economists. The politics of land use can be either statist or individualistic. For example, Sunstein would increase the power and scope of the regulatory state. Malloy, on the other hand, would cut back the regulatory state and prefers natural rights approach to takings.

At the abstract philosophical level, Honore presents a view of "ownership" that does not let the object fall out of the property relation. If the object of the relation drops out or is neglected, then the notion of property becomes empty. Grunebaum, on the other hand, believe that the word "property" is too metaphysical and should be dropped. He would substitute the word "ownership" as being a more accurate and broader reflection of the real world uses of property than are captured by the word "property."

The relation between the state and protection of private property from unjustified interference is a mainstay of American civil society. The various permutations—nuisance, substantive due process, liberty of contract, and takings—are the manifestations of a society that places property at the top of the constitutional structure of government. However, the Supreme Court ran into trouble attempting to give exclusive protection to private property to the exclusion of other values, during the Depression era.

The balancing of interests approach has its own set of problems. Utilitarian analysis and balancing of interests presumes that interests can be quantified in some way. This makes for settling disputes by reaching a median point. Whether this is "fair" or a "just" outcome for the disputants is not a priority because one value is not seen as superior to another value. Justice is reaching a median point. This is different from the *per se* rule following perspective—violation of a rule is indicative of guilt.

The compensation component of takings, again, is a difficult determination. What is "fair" compensation for governmental interference with private property is not obvious. Whether market value is the best measure is a debatable point. Even a Chicago School conservative—Richard Epstein—is unsure that markets capture all of the value taken in takings cases. Conservatives and libertarians want to maximize the compensation award for property taken or interfered with by regulation or condemnation. By making it too expensive for government to pursue regulations and acquisitions of property, they hope to force government to give up its efforts. Liberals are inclined to allow for greater government regulation of private property.

The courts, being a branch of the state, have the responsibility of taking general legislation and applying it to individual cases. But as this study has shown, when the Federal government does not get involved in local politics, Federal courts become confused when left to their own devices. The Supreme Court, as shown in the land use arena, has not been able for the most part to achieve anything better than *ad hoc* solutions.

It is important that local governments continue to have an important say as to local matters but not devoid of the Federal government. Otherwise, excessive localism reduces itself to parochialism and tribalism. Further, it is not productive if local governments have the only say in land use policy because local problems have general implications. And local governments are not in the best position to assess the general implications of local land management. Under the existing land use system, there are problems of coordination, efficiency, and bargaining costs that lead to less than optimal results. Dealing with thousands of fiefdoms is not conducive to building a united America. History tells us that excessive local controls can be detrimental to building a broader community and can be a source for bloodshed.

Currently, property rights groups are vying to deliver the death blow to the New Deal regulatory state—that is, the deregulation of property interests under the banner of over-taxation and over-regulation. Those that are pushing for the wholesale dismantling of the Federal government must assume that markets can police themselves and markets are the solution to the nation's civil and property ills. This work has argued that markets cannot provide social and political solution nor serve as a substitute for the political process as the radical libertarians are prone to believe. This work has argued that it is utopian to believe that markets are the solution to political questions. To be sure markets are an important ingredient in our system and markets certainly have produced a standard of living for most Americans that is the envy of the world.

Further, these property rights groups have erred in targeting the New Deal as the cause of modern social problems. Although the New Deal gave shape to the modern regulatory state, its roots lie within the American Constitution. The foundation of the modern American state lies in the Madisonian compound republic. The structure of our Constitution sets the parameters of the modern state. A unitary state structure would have significantly reduced the level of government, but the Founders rejected the unitary state for the compound state. Of course, at the close of the eighteenth and throughout the nineteenth century all levels of government were minimal in comparison with today. However, the people of those centuries lived in a world vastly different from our own. History can teach us important lessons but does not let us do it over again.

In the spirit of learning from history, it may be the case that the moderns may have missed some important lessons. The ancients may have understood something about the barbarity of human nature that modern psychology has blunted. That is, the psycholgisms of the day speak to the treatment and reformation of our species, perhaps a byproduct of the Judeo-Christian theology, and overlook the fact that not all are susceptible to reform. This has lead to the civil deterioration of our society. Of course, this would not be the sole cause for such a deterioration. But the severity of penalties and exactions that a society draws from the criminal element is an integral component of the life that we make for ourselves.

In a utopian world, courts can render perfect justice to the aggrieved, but in a less than perfect world the dispensation of perfect justice always falls short. The best we can hope for is workable justice given our knowledge, resources, and social conditions. The philosophic question that modern courts face is how to dispense "fair" justice to each individual and at the same time apply general principles of law? How is a judge to render the general particular? This has deep philosophical roots. It may be the case that the way the question is posed has no real solutions. But the substance of the problem is real, although its phrasing is susceptible to re-subscription.

In the property arena, the Supreme Court answered the general/particular question wrongly. Because it addressed the *ad hoc* part of the question, the individual case, but fell far short of coming to grips with the general part of the question—albeit without much help from the other branches of government. But philosophers have also failed to break out of the prevailing linguistic grip. Certainly, the relation of word to thing and naming play important role in how problems are approached. But the connection between the word and the thing has to be real at some foundational level; otherwise, we would exist in some psychotic universe. Analytic philosophers seem to have thrown overboard this connection. It would seem that if movement and action are the natural state of the world and inactivity and the stationary are not real, this allows us to re-conceive how the word functions with respect to the object; by naming, words function in making general and stable the particular and the transitory.

As far as the word "property" is concerned, it makes general the nominal, not is some absolute sense, but in the demarcation of an underlying universe of motion. Because of the underlying stream of change and universal motion, the coordination and correspondence between the word and the object does not present a perfect match that will be stable for all times and all places. But this does not mean that the atomic and sub-atomic world is beyond naming nor arbitrary because we are unable to get the word to capture nature in a stationary state. Where philosophers make the mistake is in believing correspondence between words and things is unattainable due to the underlying flow of physical matter. However, we do not live nor work in the subatomic world. The relations of the subatomic world are not applicable to the day to day social world. So it is a mistake to apply the rules and behavior of atomic particles to the world of as we know, experience, and live it.

Takings law overall remains in a muddle. Various cases have been handed down by the Supreme Court in an attempt to solve these property issues. Most Supreme Court observers remain unsatisfied with the results. The various theorists, discussed here, attempted to generate constructive criticism and suggest various alternatives as to how to deal with takings problems. If this work makes a small contribution to the ongoing debates, it would be in its interdisciplinary approach to takings law and property issues. That is, if this work has any value, it will be in approaching the problem from an integrative perspective that crosses discipline lines and does not treat the problems in isolation.

NOTES

PART I

CHAPTER ONE: ORIGIN OF THE TAKINGS CLAUSE

1. Article 29 (1225) in Bosselman, Fred, David Callies, & John Banta, *The Taking Issue*, pp. 56, 53–58; Bender, "The Takings Clause: Principles or Politics?," p. 50.
2. Sackman, Julius L. & Patrick J. Rohan, *Nichols' The Law of Eminent Domain*, Sect. 1.12.
3. Bosselman et al., p. 93.
4. Platt, Rutherford H., *Land Use Control: Geography, Law, and Public Policy*, p. 51.
5. Platt, pp. 44,51.
6. Treanor, "The Origins and Original Significance of the Just Compensation Clause of the Fifth Amendment," p. 695; Treanor's more recent views can be found in, "The Original Understanding of the Takings Clause and the Political Process."
7. Treanor, p. 701; for a general discussion of the overall thrust of the period, whether liberal or republican, *see*: Hartz, Louis, *The Liberal Tradition in America: An Interpretation of American Political Thought since the Revolution*; Wood, Gordon, *The Creation of the American Republic, 1877–1787*; Pocock, J.G.A., *The Machiavellian Moment: Florentine Political Thought and the Atlantic Republican Tradition*.
8. Bosselman et al., p. 104; Ackerman, Bruce A., *Private Property and the Constitution*, p. 192n.10.
9. Bosselman et al., p. 115n.26.
10. *Barron v. Baltimore*, 32 U.S. (7 Pet.) 243 (1833).
11. Treanor, p. 701.
12. Horwitz, Morton J., *The Transformation of American Law 1780–1860*, p. 31.
13. Horwitz, p. 31; *see also*, Friedman, Lawrence M., *American Law*, pp. 51–55; Fawcett, "Eminent Domain, The Police Power, and The Fifth Amendment: Defining the Domain of the Takings Analysis," pp. 494–495; Orren, "Labor Regulation and Constitutional Theory in The United States and England." (Karen Orren believes that Horwitz is essentially correct. Her views only differ slightly. "Here our picture differs slightly from the now familiar one of antebellum courts actively promoting economic activity at the expense of older legal precedents." p. 107).
14. Horwitz, p. 32.
15. Horwitz, p. 39.

16. Horwitz, p. 66.
17. Although some of Horwitz's claims have an air of conspiratorial theory of judges redistributing property from static to dynamic enterprises and minimizing the compensation offered to "old" forms of property, there is a grain of truth in his description of an economic force in play that would later in the century transform the American economy from agrarian to industrial. But whether Horwitz's linear progression of history or narrative is correct is difficult to say. Although his outline and description of American property law is correct, whether the inferences he draws from this are also correct is another matter. This writer believes such inferences should be left open for further investigation. On the conspiratorial point, *see*: Smith, (Book Review), "The Transformation of American Law," p. 1253 (1977).
18. Horwitz, pp. 71–72.
19. Horwitz, p. 73; *see also*, Reznick, (Comment), "Land Use Regulation and the Concept of Takings in Nineteenth Century America," pp. 866–7.

CHAPTER TWO: THE SHAPING OF THE MODERN AMERICAN STATE

1. *Slaughter House Cases*, 83 U.S. 57 (1873).
2. *Slaughter House Cases*, 83 U.S. at 83; *see also*, Sachman, "The Right to Condemn," pp. 184–185. He says:

> In the early days, the "use value" concept was adhered to. Thus, in the *Slaughter House Cases* the majority of the Supreme Court held that the statute there in question did not affect a deprivation of property as the term is used in the Fourteenth Amendment, Mr. Justice Miller, speaking for the majority, held that the term "property," as used in the due process clause, retained its common law meaning of physical things held exclusively for one's use. It meant "use value," not "exchange value." However, even in that case, one of the dissenters, Mr. Justice Swayne, said: "Property is everything which has exchangeable value, and the right of property includes the power to dispose of it according to the will of the owner." (Sachman, pp. 184–5).

3. Sachman, "The Right to Condemn," p. 185. According to Sackman, "title and possession" of physical property could be taken for public use, under eminent domain, but "only on condition that equivalent value should be paid," or just compensation, and this was a judicial question. (paraphrasing Sachman).

4. Sachman, p. 186; *see also*, Reznick, (Comment), "Land Use Regulation and the Concept of Takings in the Nineteenth Century" (1973).

5. Sachman, p. 188.

6. Reznick, (Comment)(1973), p. 856.

7. Reznick, (Comment)(1973), p. 857.

8. The power of Eminent Domain is the inherent power of the sovereign to take property for a public use with compensation without the need to obtain the permission of the property owner. *See*, Gifis, Steven H., *Law Dictionary*, p. 153.

9. 91 U.S. 367 (1875).

10. The point being made is that the Federal government did not begin to fully assert itself until after the Civil War. The following factors contributed to shifting of power away from the States to the Federal government. These are: 1) the Civil War, 2) the increased pace of industrialization, and 3) the problems of urbanization. The Supreme Court contributed to transferring more power to the Federal government by the way it interpreted the Civil War Amendments—in particular the Fourteenth Amendment. It was found that it incorporated certain portions of the Bill of Rights, making those portions of the Bill of Rights applicable and enforceable against the States. Of course, the process that is being described was not a uniform or instantaneous accomplishment. I only point to the origin. This process of transferring more power to the Federal government would take many decades to work itself through, and it continued well into the Twentieth century. For an explanation of the expanding role of the judiciary in the protection of property during this period; *see*, Paul, A.M., *Conservative Crises and the Rule of Law*, pp. 2, 41–42.

11. 166 U.S. 226 (1897).

12. *Nichols' The Law of Eminent Domain* Sect. 6.05.

13. 80 U.S. (13 Wall.) 166 (1871).

14. *Pumpelly*, 80 U.S. at 181.

15. Reznick, (Comment), "Land Use Regulation and the Concept of Takings in the Nineteenth Century," (1973), p. 867.

16. 188 U.S. 445 (1903).

17. *Lynah*, 188 U.S. at 469.

18. 192 U.S. 217 (1904).

19. As indicated, the Court has a checkered history of applying consequential damages. Again, the Court in *Peabody v. United States*, 231 U.S. 530 (1913), refused to expand takings based on consequential damages, e.g., firing heavy guns over the plaintiff's property. The facts of this case bar a taking because the guns were only fired for testing and not on a continuous

basis. The Court, however, stated in *dicta* that if the government installed the guns with the intent to practice regularly over the plaintiff's property—"with intent of depriving the owner of its profitable use"—then this could be a taking.

In *Portsmouth Harbor Land & Hotel Co. v. United States*, 250 U.S. 1 (1919), a hotel owner sought recovery due to firings of battery. Justice Holmes adopted what was *dicta* in *Peabody*, ordering that evidence be presented to see if repeated firings were sufficient to prove intent to create a servitude over the hotel property. It was found that the government took a servitude over the property due to additional firings of the battery.

20. Reznick, (Comment), "Land Use Regulations and the Concept of Takings in the Nineteenth Century," (1973), p. 868; *see also*, Bender, "The Takings Clause: Principles or Politics?," p. 765; Bosselman *et al.*, pp. 115–117.

21. *Pumpelly, Lynah, Portsmouth Harbor, United States v. Welch*, 217 U.S. 133 (1910) (permanent flooding of land for right of way constituted a taking); *United States v. Crest*, 243 U.S. 316 (1917) (direct invasion of land by flooding constituted a taking).

22. 123 U.S. 623 (1887).

23. The police power is defined as:

> Police power is a state's inherent authority to regulate for the health, welfare, safety, and morals of its citizens. The fifth and fourteenth amendments to the Constitution limit that otherwise absolute power by requiring that all police power measures that deprive a person of life, liberty, or property conform to the due process standards. (Bender, p. 764).

Bender claims that the phrase "police power" was coined by Chief Justice Marshall in *Brown v. Maryland*, 25 U.S. (12 Weat.) 419, 433 (1827) (*see* Bender, p. 764 footnote).

More will be said about this power in the next section. However, this phrase "police power" is a misnomer by modern standard usage. Some have attempted to re-label this power to better describe what it does, but it will not be re-labeled here, since it is too ingrained in constitutional law discourse, and the use of other equivalent terms could lead to misunderstanding.

24. *Mugler*, 123 U.S. at pp. 668–669.

25. Large, "The Supreme Court and the Takings Clause: The Search for a Better Rule," (1987), pp. 8–9.

26. Large, p. 9; Lipsker & Heldt, "Regulatory Takings: A Contract," (1988), p. 211.

27. Reznick, (Comment), "Land Use Regulations and the Concept of Takings in the Nineteenth Century," (1973), p. 854; for an early interpretation of the police power in a non-land use context *see*, *License Cases*, 46 U.S. 504, 589 (1847).
28. Bender, "Takings Clause: Principles or Politics?," (1985), p. 764; Freund, Ernest, *The Police Power, Public Policy and Constitutional Rights* (1904); *Nichols' The Law of Eminent Domain*, Sect. 1.42.
29. Freund, p. iii.
30. Freund, p. 65; *see also*, *License Cases*, 46 U.S. 504 (1847); *Legal Tender Cases*, 12 Wall. 457, 551 (1871) (no taking due to devaluation in the "greenback").
31. Freund, pp. 546–9.
32. Freund, pp. 546–547; *see also*,

> In the exercise of eminent domain property or an easement therein is taken from the owner and applied to the public use because the use or enjoyment of such property or easement is beneficial to the public. In the exercise of the police power the owner is denied the unrestricted use or enjoyment of the property that is injurious to the public welfare. Under the police power the property is not, as a general rule, appropriated to another use, but is destroyed or its value impaired, while under the power of eminent domain its transferred to the state to be enjoyed and used by it as its own. (*Nichols' The Law of Eminent Domain*, Sect. 6.05).

33. Freund, p. 549.
34. Freund, pp. 550–551.
35. 239 U.S. 394 (1915).
36. Sax, "Takings and The Police Power," (1964) p. 39. Sax:

> Thus the Harlan theories distinguish takings from exercises of the police power by artful definition of the terms "taking" and "property." Under the Harlan, theory the constitutional question never turns upon an examination of the economic consequences of the government's action; these theories postulate a qualitative difference between the police power and a taking, not a mere difference of degree. (Sax, p. 39).

37. *See*, Tiedman, Christopher G., *A Treatise on The Limitation of Police Power in the United States* (1886) p. 424. For a brief biography of Tiedman and re-examination of his version of laissez-faire constitutionalism, *see*, Halper, Louise A., "Christopher G. Tiedman, 'Laissez-Faire Constitutionalism' and the Dilemmas of Small-Scale Property in the Gilded Age," p. 1349 (1990).
38. Large, p. 10.
39. McGinley, "Regulatory "Takings": The Remarkable Resurrection of Economic Substantive Due Process," (1988) p. 344.

40. *Munn v. Illinois*, 94 U.S. 113 (1877).
41. McGinley, p. 351.
42. *Munn*, 94 U.S. at 84. Justice Waite writing for the Court said:

> Looking, then, to the common law, from whence came the right which
> the Constitution protects, we find that when private property is "affected
> with a public interest, it ceases to be *juris privati* only." This was said by
> Lord Chief Justice Hale more than two hundred years ago, in his treatise
> *De Portibus Maris* and has been accepted without objection as an
> essential element in the law of property ever since. Property does not
> become clothed with a public interest when used in a manner to make it
> of public consequence, and affected the community at large. When,
> therefore, one devotes his property to a use in which the public has an
> interest in that use, and must submit to be controlled by the public for the
> common good, to the extent of the interest he has thus created. He may
> withdraw his grant by discontinuing the use; but, so long as he maintains
> the use, he must submit to the control. (*Munn*, p. 84).

43. *Munn*, 94 U.S. at 8.
44. *Munn*, 94 U.S. at 88. (Justice Field dissenting).
45. *Munn*, 94 U.S. at 89 (Justice Field dissenting).
46. *Munn*, 94 U.S. at 90 (Justice Field dissenting).
47. Carr, R.K., *The Supreme Court and Judicial Review* (1942) p. 146.
    Carr put it this way:

> The conservative minority in the Court gained in strength during the late
> 1870's and 1880's. These were the years in which the Industrial
> Revolution made tremendous headway in the United States, with the
> result that conservative business points of view were of considerable
> importance and came to have an increasing influence upon the
> government. In many ways, business interests sought special favors and
> positive action from legislatures. But in good part, the interest of business
> was to avoid government regulation. (Carr, p. 146).

48. 134 U.S. 970 (1890).
49. *Chicago, Milwaukee*, 134 U.S. at 971.
50. Paul, A.M., *Conservative Crises and the Rule of Law: Attitudes of
    Bar and Bench, 1887–1895* (1960) pp. 41–42. Paul states that
    Chicago, Milwaukee was pivotal in the rise of the new
    constitutionalism. Although *Munn* was still unrepealed, says
    Paul, "it was in danger of being outflanked," and the door was
    being opened for "judicial supervision of state regulation on the
    grounds of reasonableness." *see also*, Frankfurter, Felix &
    Henry M. Hart, Jr., "Rate Regulation," in *The Crises of the
    Regulatory Commissions*.

51. McGinley, "Regulatory "Takings,"" (1988), pp. 351–2. McGinley said:

> Jurists and commentators who shared their concern about the breadth of the holding in *Munn* cast about for some theory that would limit legislative exercise of the police power. Their search led to theories such as that of Justice Brewer, in which regulatory initiatives that set rates so low that a "fair return" on investment could not be realized ought to be judicially rejected as the virtual equivalent of physical confiscation of property. (McGinley, pp. 351–2).

McGinley is referring to Justice Brewer's defense of private property in particular *Budd v. State of New York*, 143 U.S. 247, 257 (1892) (Justice Brewer, dissenting).

Finally, in 1898, the Court ended the dispute as to what is a "fair return."

> After two decades of controversy and analytical gestation, in *Smyth v. Ames* (1898) the Supreme Court announced a test that stood for 40 years as the rule by which rate regulation could be distinguished from confiscation. The touchstone of *Smyth v. Ames* was a "fair return" on the "fair value" of a railroad's property. (McGinley, p. 352).

52. *Lochner v. New York*, 198 U.S. 45 (1905) (case involved the number of hours bakers could work); *see also*, Paul, A.M., *Conservative Crises and the Rule of Law*, p. 2. Paul said:

> As popular discontent grew more menacing in the 1890's, and conservative alarm for the security of property increased accordingly, the role of courts assumed a new importance. Gradually at first, and then with rapid strides, the judiciary emerged in the mid 1890's as the principal bulwark of conservative defense. The transformation of the due process clause into a substantive check upon the legislative regulation, the development of the labor injunction as an anti-strike weapon, the near-emasculation of the Sherman Anti-Trust Act in the *E.C. Knight* case, and the overthrow of the federal income tax in the *Pollock* case were related aspects of a massive judicial entry into the socio-economic scene. American constitutionalism underwent a revolution in the 1890's, a conservative-oriented revolution which vastly expanded the scope of judicial supremacy, with important consequences for American economic and political history. (Paul, A.M., p. 2).

> and, *see generally*, Gillman, Howard, *The Constitution Besieged: The Rise and Demise of Lochner Era Police Power Jurisprudence* (1993).

53. McGinley, p. 353.
54. Schultz, David A., *Property, Power, and American Democracy*, (1992), p. 47.

The period 1867–1937 represented both the "ascendancy and decline" of the (contract) clause. It was a period of ascendancy because except for the Commerce clause, no other clause was used more often by the Court to invalidate state legislation. In general, the clause's usage declined as the police power and substantive due process doctrines evolved to limit and replace the clause as a defender of private property. (Schultz, p. 47).

55. Schultz, p. 54. Further, in the 1930's, due to economic conditions and F.D.R.'s New Deal, pressure was applied to the Court to re-define what it meant to take property. The Court's essentially narrow common law reading of property yielded to statutory redefinition of what property meant. Schultz put it this way:

Finally, the redefinition of reasonableness was changed from the existing standard—not impinging one's economic rights—to a new standard—does the statute further the health, safety, morals, and welfare of the community? By changing the standard of reasonableness the Court would use, the Court overruled half of *Mugler* and return to the legislature the right to be the judge over the reasonableness of regulation. This is what happened in *Carolene Products*. (Schultz, p. 54).

The Supreme Court believed that much of the New Deal legislation took property and was redistributive. But under continuous pressure, the Court yielded in *Home Building and Loan Association v. Blaisdell*, 290 U.S. 398 (1934) (1933 Minnesota Moratorium Law that provided for a two year emergency moratorium on foreclosures of real estate property).

CHAPTER THREE: THE BEGINNING OF MODERN TAKINGS LAW

1. 260 U.S. 393 (1922).
2. Bosselman, *et al.*, *The Taking Issue* (1973).
3. Lipsker & Heldt, "Regulatory Takings: A Contract," (1988), p. 214.
4. Lipsker & Heldt, p. 215.
5. Lipsker & Heldt, p. 216.
6. Lipsker & Heldt, p. 213.

The 1922 landmark case of *Pennsylvania Coal Co. v. Mahon* is the source of most of the regulatory takings tests utilized by the courts today. Justice Holmes laid the groundwork for the variety of tests: a confiscating test, a substantial interference with use test, a diminished value test, and a reciprocity of advantage test. All involve the extent to which there is an interference with the freedom of use rather than with possession. (Lipsker & Held, p. 213).

7. Lawrence, "Regulatory Takings: Beyond the Balancing Test," (1988), p. 396.

8. Connors, "Back to the Future: The "Nuisance Exception" to the Just Compensation Clause," (1989), pp. 162–163.

9. Lawrence, p. 397.

10. 232 U.S. 531 (1914).

11. Coletta, "Reciprocity of Advantage and Regulatory Takings: Toward a New Theory of Takings Jurisprudence," (1990), p. 311.

12. Coletta, p. 313.

13. Coletta, p. 303.

14. Coletta, p. 319.

15. Coletta, p. 322.

16. Lipsker & Heldt, p. 214.

17. Lawrence, pp. 397–398.

18. *Pennsylvania Coal*, 260 U.S. at 416.

19. McGinley, pp. 356–357.

20. McGinley, pp. 356–357. (McGinley's argument is not persuasive. Although a few years after *Pennsylvania Coal*, there was something of a return to *Mugler* type analysis in the case of *Miller v. Schoene*, 276 U.S. 272 (1928), *Pennsylvania Coal* would ultimately dictate takings law.)

21. Linowers, R. Robert & Don T. Allensworth, *The Politics of Land-Use: Developers vs. Citizens Groups in the Courts* (1976), p. 43.

22. Williams & Taylor, eds. *Williams American Planning Law: Land Use and The Police Power*, (1988 revision), Chapter 5, pp. 103–104.

23. 272 U.S. 365 (1926).

24. Williams & Taylor, p. 105.

25. Williams & Taylor, p. 106.

26. Williams & Taylor, pp. 103–106; *see also*, Linowers & Allensworth, p. 44.

27. Anderson, Robert M., *American Law of Zoning* 3d, Chapter 3, p. 92.

28. Anderson, p. 95.

29. Anderson, p. 97.

30. Anderson, p. 107.

31. 272 U.S. 365 (1926).

32. *Euclid*, 272 U.S. at 384.

33. *Euclid*, 272 U.S. at 389.

34. ·*Euclid*, 272 U.S. at 388. "If the validity of the legislative classification for zoning purposes be fairly debatable, the legislative judgment must be allowed to control." (p. 288)

Linowers and Allensworth believe that the fairly debatable standard is problematic. "The problem with the fairly debatable principle is that it has little meaning in practical settings, and the tendency is for courts to uphold a wide variety of zoning actions

on these grounds because almost any zoning question is fairly debatable." (Linowers & Allensworth, p. 44).
35. Linowers & Allensworth, pp. 48–49.

> [N]o zoning litigation reached the high body between *Nectow* (1928) and *Hempstead* (1962), or between *Hempstead* and *Belle Terre*, considered in 1974. [P]erhaps the dominant pattern over these years was for the court to avoid the land-use field altogether, some may say assiduously so. A 1954 case, *Berman v. Parker*, is important to land-use scholars, planners, zoning attorneys, and others in the field, but it involved urban renewal and not zoning per se. (Linowers & Allensworth, pp. 48–49).

36. *Nectow v. City of Cambridge*, 277 U.S. 183 (1928).
37. *Nectow*, 277 U.S. at 187.
38. *Nectow*, 277 U.S. at 188.

CHAPTER FOUR: THE SUPREME COURT ABANDONS LAND USE LAW

1. A condemnation proceeding is a formal declaration by the government that it intends to exercise its power of eminent domain.
2. *See*, the following cases: *Home Building and Loan Association v. Blaisdell*, 290 U.S. 398 (1934); *West Coast Hotel Co. v. Parrish*, 300 U.S. 379 (1937); *United States v. Carolene Products Co.*, 304 U.S. 144 (1938).

   For a general analysis of judicial review and politics, *see*, Sunstein, "Naked Preferences and the Constitution," (1984).

   Substantive due process, in the economic/property sphere, has been de-emphasized since the time of Justice Stone's *Carolene Products* opinion. Footnote four of that opinion became more famous than the case itself.

   See also, Nedelsky, "American Constitutionalism and the Paradox of Private Property," pp. 241, 247–8.

   Since the late 1930's the Court has not *checked* the legislature effectively in the property/economic domain. In the labor law context Karen Orren says that:

   > In the United States, in the half century following the Court's upholding of the Wagner Act, no social policy of Congress was significantly reversed by the judiciary—with a single exception that revealed, in its rapid turnabout, the legislative tow beneath. Let the farewell to the old regime belong to a rueful Justice Roberts, denouncing his brethren's generous reading of the Norris LaGuardia anti-injunction statute "a process of construction never [h]eretofore indulged by this court." Prior

to the New Deal, of course, there had been no contradiction between a nonsovereign American legislature in practice and a nonsovereign American legislature in theory. Afterwards, with the legislature's victory in practice, there would appear the "counter-majoritarian difficulty" and the thrashing around by present-day jurists for some new (and narrow) theoretical basis for judicial review. (Orren, *Labor Regulation and Constitutional Theory In The United States and England*, pp. 116–117).

3. 148 U.S. 312 (1893).
4. *Monogahela*, 148 U.S. at 327.
5. *Monogahela*, 148 U.S. at 328.
6. *Monogahela*, 148 U.S. at 328.
7. *Monogahela*, 148 U.S. at 329.
8. *See, Omnia Commercial Co. v. United States*, 261 U.S. 502 (1923). (Omnia had a contract to purchase steel plate. The United States government requisitioned the steel plate during World War I. According to *Monogahela*, this action should lead to compensation. But in this case the Court did not find a taking because the taking was indirect. It was consequential. That is, the government took over the factory that produced the steel plate rather than abrogate the contract directly.)

     See also, Danforth v. United States, 308 U.S. 271 (1939) (This case fixes the point that interest starts to accrue. Danforth's land was flooded due to work done on the levees. The Court held that interest starts to accrue at the time of the taking. Danforth wanted to start collecting interest from the time the legislation was passed to take the property. The Court ruled that only when the government appropriates or uses the property does the interest start to accrue.)

9. *United States v. General Motors Corp.*, 323 U.S. 373 (1945).
10. *General Motors*, 323 U.S. at 379.
11. *General Motors*, 323 U.S. at 382.
12. 338 U.S. 1 (1949).
13. *Kimball*, 338 U.S. at 5.
14. *Kimball*, 338 U.S. at 9.
15. Other cases add and clarify what is consequential and what is directly included in a compensation package. For example, in *United States v. Commodities Trading Corp.*, 339 U.S. 121 (1950), whole black pepper was requisitioned by the Department of War in 1944—put a ceiling price it will pay—the Court said that the government is not required to compensate for the loss of potential profits.

     United States v. Dow, 357 U.S. 17 (1958) (Court clarifies issues of who should be compensated if there has been a change in ownership from the time the government announced that it will take the property to the time of the actual taking. Again, it is to compensate the owner at the time of the actual taking of possession.)

16. Comment, "The Public Use Limitation on Eminent Domain: An Advance Requiem," (1949), p.610. *See also*, Sachman, "The Right to Condemn," (1965), p. 182. Sachman claims that the word "use" is susceptible to two different meanings: employment and advantage. Under the narrow reading "use" is read as "used by the public" literally. (p. 182) Sachman claims that under a broad reading, "public use" means "public advantage" such as "enlarge the resources, increase the industrial energies, and promote the productive power of any considerable number of inhabitants of a section of the state." (p. 182)

    See also, Hoff, "Development of the Concept of Eminent Domain," (1942), pp. 598–599.

17. 348 U.S. 26 (1954).

18. Sachman, p. 183; *see also*, Paul, Ellen F., "Public Use: A Vanishing Limitation on Government Takings," p. 360.

19. Paul, Ellen F., "Public Use," p. 360.

20. Paul, Ellen F., "Public Use," p. 361. The case she is referring to is *United States ex rel. Tennessee Valley Authority v. Welch*, 327 U.S. 546 (1946). She claims that it was cases like *Welch* and *United States v. Gettysburg Electric R. Co.*, 160 U.S. 668 (1896), that paved the way to interpreting "public use" broadly. (Paul, E.F., p. 362) In *Gettysburg* the Court claimed that what is a "public use" is a legislative question, but Paul claims that in *Cincinnati v. Vester* (281 U.S. 439 (1930)), what is a "public use" was a judicial question.

21. Paul, Ellen F., "Public Use," pp. 363–364.

22. Bender, "The Takings Clause," p. 780.

23. Bender, p. 825.

24. Fawcett, "Eminent Domain, the Police Power and the Fifth Amendment," p. 498.

25. Fawcett, p. 499.

26. Dunham, "*Griggs v. Alleghany County* in Perspective: Thirty Years of Supreme Court Expropriation Law," (1962), p. 66.

27. Dunham, pp. 66–67.

28. Dunham, p. 71.

29. *See also*, the following cases on public use questions: *United States ex rel. T.V.A. v. Welch* (1946); *Ridge Co. v. Los Angeles*, 262 U.S. 700 (1923); *Mt. Vernon Cotton Co. v. Alabama Power Co.*, 240 U.S. 30 (1916).

30. 82 S. Ct. 987 (1962).

31. *Goldblatt*, 82 S. Ct. at 988.
32. *Goldblatt*, 82 S. Ct. at 989.
33. *Goldblatt*, 82 S. Ct. at 989.
34. *Goldblatt*, 82 S. Ct. at 990.

> The question, therefore, narrows to whether the prohibition of further excavation below the water table is a valid exercise of the town's police power. The term "police power" connotes the time-tested conceptional limit of public encroachment upon private interests. Except for the substitution of the familiar standard of "reasonableness," this Court has generally refrained from announcing any specific criteria. (*Goldblatt*, p. 990).

There is no set formula to determine where regulation ends and taking begins. (p. 987)

35. *Goldblatt*, 82 S. Ct. at 990.

> The ordinance in question was passed as a safety measure, and the town is attempting to uphold it on that basis. To evaluate its reasonableness we therefore need to know such things as the nature of the menace against which it will protect, the availability and effectiveness of other less drastic protective steps, and the loss which appellants will suffer from the imposition of the ordinance. (*Goldblatt*, p. 990).

CHAPTER FIVE: THE RENAISSANCE OF LAND USE

1. 405 U.S. 538 (1972). This opinion was applied at lower court levels. And the unity between civil rights and property rights was rejected. For lower court application of *Lynch, see, Florida Rock Industries, Inc. v. United States*, 8 Cl. Ct. 160 (1985), *rev.*, 741 F.2d 893 (Fed. Cir. 1986).
2. 42 U.S.C. Sect. 1983 is a civil rights statute authorized under the Fourteenth Amendment.
3. *Lynch*, 405 U.S. at 552.
4. 416 U.S. 1 (1974).
5. *Village of Belle Terre*, 416 U.S. at 9.
6. In *Moore v. East Cleveland*, 431 U.S. 494 (1977), the Court will back off somewhat as to restrictions of living together with respect to extended family relationships. For an analysis of *Moore*, in relation to land use, *see*: Williams, "Euclid's Lochnerian Legacy."
7. 483 U.S. 104; 985 S. Ct. 2646.
8. *Penn Central*, 483 U.S. at 124–126; 98 S. Ct. at 2659.
9. *Penn Central*, 483 U.S. at 129–130; 98 S. Ct. at 2660–2661.
10. *Penn Central*, 483 U.S. at 129–132; 98 S. Ct. at 2662.
11. *Penn Central*, 483 U.S. at 123–125; 98 S. Ct. at 2659.

12. *Penn Central*, 483 U.S. at 133–137; 98 S. Ct. at 2664–2665.
13. *Penn Central*, 483 U.S. at 145–146; 98 S. Ct. at 2670 (Justice Rehnquist dissenting).
14. 444 U.S. 164 (1979).
15. *Kaiser Aetna*, 444 U.S. at 179–180. The Court goes on to indicate that the right to exclude is not absolute in the case of *Prune Yard Shopping Center v. Robins*, 447 U.S. 74 (1980). A couple of students were soliciting, in the Prune Yard Shopping Center, for signatures from customers, regarding a petition in opposition to a United Nations resolution. A security guard asked them to leave because it was the policy of the shopping center not to allow visitors to engage in activity other than commercial. Justice Rehnquist writing for the Court again recognized the right to exclude as fundamental. However, unlike *Kaiser Aetna*, the physical invasion here was temporary and *de minimis*. *See also*, *Radiooptics, Inc. v. United States*, 621 F. 2d 1113 (1980).
16. 444 U.S. 51 (1979).
17. *Andrus*, 444 U.S. at 52.
18. *Andrus*, 444 U.S. at 66.
19. 447 U.S. 255 (1980).
20. *Agins*, 447 U.S. at 258n.2; 100 S. Ct. at 2140n2.
21. *Agins*, 447 U.S. at 259–261; 100 S. Ct. at 2141.
22. *Agins*, 447 U.S. at 259–263; 100 S. Ct. at 2141–2142.
23. Williams & Ernst, "And Now We Are Here On a Darkling Plain," (1989), p. 164n.56.
24. *Agins*, 447 U.S. at 261–263; 100 S. Ct. at 2142.
25. *Agins*, 447 U.S. at 261–163; 100 S. Ct. at 2142.
26. *Agins*, 447 U.S. at 261–163; 100 S. Ct. at 2142–2143.
27. In 1981, the Court decided *Hodel v. Virginia Surface Mining & Reclamation Assn., Inc.*, 452 U.S. 264 (1981). The Court procrastinated in reaching a decision in inverse condemnation and temporary takings law. It side stepped the issue by finding a procedural defect. Virginia had passed the Surface Mining Control and Reclamation Act of 1977. Virginia Surface was an association of coal producers. Hodel was Secretary of the Interior. The purpose of the Act was to protect society and the environment from the adverse effects of surface mining. The association brought a suit for a violation of the Commerce Clause, equal protection, and substantive due process violations. The District Court found no such violation, but it did find a violation of the 10th Amendment. That is, an interference by Congress in matters that are traditionally left to the States. But, the Supreme Court rejected the District Court's characterization because the environmental effects of surface mining were

regional and not confined to each State or end at the border of each State.

What the legislation required was that the mine owners return the site back to its "approximate original contour." The Court was unable to decide the substantive issues in the case because of a procedural defect. That is, the facial challenge was not ripe for decision—that it did not present a concrete instance. (pp. 295–296) The mere enactment of the Act is not a taking itself. (pp. 295–296) This was a repeat of *Agins*. Here, as in *Agins*, the Act had a legitimate state purpose and was not to be defeated facially.

28. 450 U.S. 621; 101 S. Ct. 1287 (1981).

29. *San Diego Gas & Electric*, 450 U.S. at 657; 101 S. Ct. at 1307 (Justice Brennan dissenting). Justice Brennan's dissent drew heated polemics. Williams, *et al.*, believe that no compensation is due or should be due for any police power regulation. Williams, Smith, Siemon, Mandelker, & Babcock, "The White River Junction Manifesto." Counter-attacking this position is Berger & Kanner, "Thoughts on the *White River Junction Manifesto*: A Reply to the "Gang of Five's" Views on Just Compensation for Regulatory Takings of Property."

30. 458 U.S. 419 (1982).

31. 467 U.S. 229 (1984).

32. 410 Mich. 616 (1981). On the one hand, General Motors threatened to leave the city of Detroit if the city did not condemn certain lands for General Motors to expand and modernize its plant. On the other hand, there are the needs of a well knit ethnic community that were the target of the condemnation. Should the City of Detroit accommodate G.M., thereby keeping the tax base and jobs in Detroit, or should it support the unity and solidarity of this Polish community? Let us not forget what is being done here. The city is seeking to condemn private property and transfer it to another private property owner. That is, the property will be used for private purposes. Nevertheless, under the broad interpretation that is given to the notion of "public use," the Supreme Court of Michigan interpreted the phrase as being equivalent to the notion of "public purpose."(p. 457) Keeping jobs in Detroit and keeping its tax base was deemed to be a public use even though the property was going to G.M.

33. *Midkiff*, 467 U.S. at 240.

34. *Midkiff*, 467 U.S. at 240.

35. *Midkiff*, 467 U.S. at 241.

36. *Midkiff*, 467 U.S. at 243–244.

37. *Midkiff*, 467 U.S. at 244.

38. *Midkiff*, 467 U.S. at 244.

39. 474 U.S. 121 (1985).

40. *United States v. Locke*, 471 U.S. 84 (1985)(unpatented mining claims requiring filing procedure).

41. 482 U.S. 304; 107 S. Ct. 2378 (1987).

42. *Nollan v. California Coastal Commission*, 483 U.S. 825; 107 S. Ct. 3141 (1987). *See further*, Sterk, Stewart E., *"Nollan*, Henry George, and Exactions," p. 1731 (1988). *See generally*, Been, Vicki, ""Exit" as a Constraint on Land Use Exactions: Rethinking the Unconstitutional Conditions Doctrine," p. 473 (1991); Kendall, Douglas T. & James E. Ryan, ""Paying" for Change: Using Exactions and Sidestep *Nollan* and *Dolan*,"(1996).

43. A lower Federal court in 1991 said that *Nollan* should not be read broadly in the case of *Leroy Land Development v. Tahoe Regional Planning Agency*, 939 F. 2d 696 (9th Cir. 1991).

44. *Keystone Bituminous Coal Association v. DeBenedictis*, 480 U.S. 470; 107 S. Ct. 1232 (1987).

45. *Keystone*, 480 U.S. at 489–490; 107 S. Ct. at 1244.

46. *Keystone*, 480 U.S. at 490–492; 107 S. Ct. at 1245.

47. *Keystone*, 480 U.S. at 498; 107 S. Ct. at 1248.

    The major non-land use case, in the 1987 blockbuster cases, was *Hodel v. Irving*, 107 S. Ct. 2076 (1987). This case is important because it shows that interfering with devise and descent laws can result in a taking. There was an extreme fractionating of Indian lands. Congress passed the Consolidation Act of 1983 to remedy the problem. But the Court found that section 207 of this Act resulted in the taking of property. The problem that Congress was attempting to remedy was one which involved increased family size over generations left smaller pieces of property to each succeeding generation. Congress wanted to consolidate these lands. Lands that were so fractured were to escheat to the tribe, but the Court found this mechanism to be a taking because it interferes with the laws of devise and descent.

48. *Yee v. City of Escondido*, 112 S. Ct. 1522 (1992); *Preseault v. I.C.C.*, 110 S. Ct. 914 (1990); *United States v. Sperry*, 110 S. Ct. 387 (1989); *Pennell v. City of San Jose*, 108 S. Ct. 849 (1988). (*Yee* is a mobile park case. California law limits a landlord's ability to disapprove incoming tenants or evict existing ones. Escondido controls rent in mobile home parks by allowing rent increases or pegging increases to the consumer price index. The park owners claimed that state restrictions and local rent control ordinances effected a physical taking of their property at below market rent. That is, the taking was akin to a *Loretto* taking. The Court found

that there was no physical taking. The Court did not decide the other substantive issues in the case because of procedural problems.)

49. 112 S. Ct. 2886 (1992). For an analysis and history of the Rehnquist doctrine that was crystallized in this case *see*, Williams, "A Narrow Escape?," (1993), p. 122.

50. *Lucas*, 112 S. Ct. at 2994n.7.

51. *Lucas*, 112 S. Ct. at 2901–2902.

52. *Dolan v. City of Tigard*, 114 S. Ct. 2309 (1994).

53. *Leroy Land Development v. Tahoe Regional Planning Agency*, 939 F. 2d 696 (9th Cir. 1991).

PART II

CHAPTER SIX: LEGAL THEORIES OF LAND USE TAKINGS

1. The word "formalism" has many connotations. It could indicate a notion of being value-neutral (Ross), of consistently applied rules (Rose-Ackerman), rules based on logic and mechanically applied (Ross, Radin), or it could signify timelessness of the underlying subject (Radin). I will indicate in the text how each of these theorists uses the term.

2. On this point, the expansion of regulation and the development of the Regulatory State *see*, Rose-Ackerman, *Rethinking the Progressive Agenda: The Reform of the American Regulatory State* (1992).

3. A play on Kant's famous distinction between Rationalistic and Empirical philosophies, between Leibnizian and Humean systems.

4. Lawrence calls this area of the law "shapeless." (Lawrence, "Regulatory Takings: Beyond the Balancing Test," (1988) p. 391. He says that modern takings doctrine is "virtually a standardless inquiry" and has produced little predictability. (p. 400)

   Ellen Frankel Paul claims that the *Pennsylvania Coal* opinion "spawned a chaotic, *ad hoc*, atheoretical pattern of decision making." (Paul, "Taking by Regulation: Resolving the Constitutional Muddle," in *Constitutional Economics* (1984) p. 199.

   Rose described the diminution-in-value test as ambiguous. (Rose, "*Mahon* Reconstructed: Why The Takings Issue Is Still a Muddle," (1984) p. 566.

Minda described the diminution-in-value test as "indeterminate and open-textured." (Minda, "The Dilemmas of Property and Sovereignty in the Postmodern Era: New Solutions for the Regulatory Takings Problem," in *Taking Property and Just Compensation* (1992) p. 155n.7).

5. Lawrence, "Regulatory Takings: Beyond the Balancing Test," (1988) p. 396.

6. Lawrence, p. 396.

7. Lawrence, p. 397.

8. Michelman, "Property, Utility, and Fairness," (1967) p. 1173.

> The concept of efficiency is, to begin with, a concept of ethical maximizing, implying the goodness of increasing some quantity to the limits of possibility—at least as long as no sacrifices are here, the concept does not focus narrowly on the total social output of tangible economic goods, or imply that this output is the quantity to be maximized. Rather, an "efficient" process is one which maximizes the total amount of welfare, of personal satisfaction, in society, and not all satisfaction is material. (Michelman, (1967) p. 1173).

9. Michelman, (1967) p. 1173. He is attempting to avoid the difficulty of measuring interpersonal utility. The difficulty was first pointed out by the economist Lionel Robbins.

10. Kaldor-Hicks is a type of efficiency whereby the gainers are able to compensate the losers and still remain gainers.

11. Michelman, (1967) pp. 1173–1174. *See also*, Mercuro & Ryan, *Law, Economics and Public Policy* (1984). They point out that the classic work of Lionel Robbins has forced economists to re-think the possibility of making interpersonal comparisons. (p. 8) And, in response to Robbin's, economists developed the compensation test. (p. 8) They say that the compensation test is a variant to Pareto optimality, which is referred to throughout the literature as the Kaldor-Hicks criterion. (p. 8) "[T]he thrust of it simply states that a policy or legal change should be sanctioned if and only if those who gain could use part of the gains to compensate the losers and still remain gainers." (p. 70)

Robbins' utility is an ordinal and not a cardinal measurement. (p. 70)

Pareto optimality presupposes the following:

> The assumption underlying, or subsumed in, the Pareto optimal (re)allocation of resources are: (1) methodological individualism; only data revealed through the choice behavior of the individual is relevant, i.e., no social values exist apart from individual values; (2) that the social welfare is defined only in terms of the welfare of individuals where social

welfare is taken to be the collective welfare or utility (ordinally measured) of the individuals who comprise the society under consideration; and (3) that the welfare of individuals within the society may not be compared, i.e., interpersonal comparisons of utility are not valid. (Mercuro & Ryan, p. 7).

See further, Fischel, "Introduction: Utilitarian Balancing and Formalism in Takings," (1988) p. 1584. (Fischel points out that the utilitarian approach of Michelman is a mixture of Pareto and Kaldor-Hicks criteria. (p. 1584))

12. Berger, "A Policy Analysis of the Taking Problem," (1974) p. 184. (Berger claims that Michelman's approach is difficult to measure and, it is based on a static model.)

13. Michelman, (1967) p. 1181.

14. Michelman, (1967) p. 2119; *see also*, Rawls, "Justice as Fairness," (1958) p. 164; for an updated and more elaborate presentation of John Rawl's theory, *see*, *A Theory of Justice* (1971).

15. Michelman attempts to balance what he calls "efficiency gains," "demoralization costs," and "settlement coats." (p. 1214) Efficiency gains are defined by Michelman as Kaldor-Hicks criterion—what the gainers are willing to pay the losers in order to carry forward a particular measure and the losers are prepared to accept. (p. 1214) Demoralization costs are the disutilities or dissatisfaction caused to losers and their sympathizers as a consequences that no compensation is offered and loss of future production or opportunities lost (social unrest) from the fact that no compensation is forthcoming. (p. 1214) Settlement costs are defined as the time, effort, and resources that would be necessary to reach settlement, so as to offset demoralization costs. (p. 1214) Based on these definitions Michelman argues that if settlement costs are less than efficiency gains and demoralization costs, then compensation should be made. (S< E+D) (p. 1215)

16. Sax, "Takings, Private Property and Public Rights," (1971); "Takings and The Police Power," (1964).

17. An example of this is *Just v. Marinette County*, 56 Wis. 2d 7 (1972).

18. Sax (1971), pp. 150–151.

19. Sax (1971), pp. 150–151.

20. Sax (1971), pp. 150–151.

21. Sax (1971), pp. 152–153.

22. Sax (1971), pp. 152–153.

23. Sax (1971), pp. 152–153 (paraphrasing Sax).

24. Sax (1971), p. 153. (This is a typical Coasean response here.)

25. Sax (1971), p. 161.

26. Costonis, "'Fair' Compensation and the Accommodation Power: Antidotes for the Taking Impasse in Land Use Controversies," (1975) p. 1022.

27. Costonis (1975) p. 1032.

28. Costonis (1975) p. 1032.

29. Costonis, "Presumptive and Per Se Takings: A Decisional Model for the Taking Issue," (1983) pp. 476–477.

30. Ross, "Modeling and Formalism in Takings Jurisprudence," (1986) p. 374.

31. Ross (1986) p. 376.

32. Ross (1986) p. 376.

33. Ross (1986) p. 375.

34. Ross (1986) pp. 376, 384, 409.

35. Ross (1986) p. 417.

36. Ross (1986) p. 374.

37. Epstein, *Takings: Private Property and the Law of Eminent Domain* (1985). For a critique of Epstein's book *see*, Sax, Book Review, "Takings," (1986) p. 286. "I am aware of no evidence, in Epstein's book or elsewhere, to suggest that the history, language, or logic of the eminent domain provision shows an intent to prevent all redistributive intervention in the economy, though the notion is central to Epstein's thesis." (p. 286) "The whole moral force—such as it is—of the book depends upon the accuracy of this simple model of a world of mine and thine and clear lines between." (p. 288) And for a more recent analysis of land use and the state, *see*, Epstein, *Bargaining with the State* (1993).

38. Epstein, *Takings* (1985)(p. 116, paraphrasing Epstein).

39. Epstein (1985) p. 116.

40. Epstein (1985) p. 116.

41. Epstein (1985) p. 116.

42. Paul, Ellen F., "Taking by Regulation: Resolving the Constitutional Muddle," in *Constitutional Economics* (1984) p. 168; *see also*, Ryan, *Property* (1987) p. 35. (Ryan claims neo-conservatives see property as the basis of liberty.)

43. Paul, E.F. (1984) p. 169.

44. Paul, E.F. (1984) p. 174.

45. Paul, E.F. (1984) p. 175–176.

46. Rose-Ackerman, *Rethinking the Progressive Agenda: The Reform of the American Regulatory State* (1992).

47. Fischel, "Introduction: Utilitarian Balancing and Formalism in Takings," (1988) p. 1595.

48. Rose-Ackerman, *Rethinking the Progressive Agenda* (1992) p. 133.

49. Rose-Ackerman (1992) p. 134.

50. Rose-Ackerman (1992) pp. 135–136. This is what Rose-Ackerman means by these elements: "private investment" asks to check a regulations effect on private investment; "insurance issue" is to determine that what is unforeseeable and hence not easily protected by insurance. If the action is unforeseeable and hence uninsurable, then it is a taking, otherwise it is not; "public investment" is to find out the economic impact of takings law on public officials. This would force public officials to take note of their regulatory scheme on the public fisc or treasury.

51. Rose-Ackerman (1992) p. 138.

52. Fischel, "Introduction," (1988) p. 1595.

53. Rose-Ackerman, "Against Ad Hockery: A Comment on Michelman," (1988) p. 1697.

54. Rose-Ackerman, "Against Ad Hockery," p. 1701.

55. Wiseman, "When The End Justifies The Means: Understanding Takings Jurisprudence In a Legal System with Integrity," (1988) p. 461.

56. Wiseman (1988) p. 465.

57. Wiseman (1988) p. 465.

58. Radin, "The Consequences of Conceptualism," (1986) p. 239.

59. Radin, "The Liberal Conception of Property: Cross Currents in the Jurisprudence of Takings," (1988).

60. Radin, "The Liberal Conception of Property," p. 1689.

61. Radin, "Property and Personhood," (1982) p. 597.

62. Radin, "The Consequences of Conceptualism," p. 239.

63. Radin, "The Liberal Conception of Property," p. 1670. She says:

> Epstein's conceptualism about property is coupled with a literalism or semantic reductionism in constitutional interpretation. It is the words of the document we are to obey, not the intent of its framers, or the result of any kind of value inquiry. Thus, in applying the fifth and fourteenth amendments we can rely on objective timeless meaning and need not grapple with subjective historical mental states or evanescent values. Articulated detailed rules that can mechanically decide individual cases are part of the obvious meaning of the word "property." Hence, according to Epstein, the application of the constitutional provisions to the vast majority of concrete cases is apparent from a reading of the document together without knowledge of the concept of property. (Radin, "The Liberal Conception of Property," p. 1670).

Radin's more recent views can be found at: "Diagnosing the Takings Problem," in *Compensatory Justice*, ed. John W. Chapman, Nomos XXXIII.

See also, Goldstein, *In Defense of the Text: Democracy and Constitutional Theory* (1991). (She presents various interpretivist readings of the Constitution).

64. Epstein, "A Last Word on Eminent Domain," (1986) p. 263.
65. Fischel, "Introduction" p. 1593.
66. Radin, "The Liberal Conception of Property," p. 1673. "In *Irving*, Justice O'Connor's opinion for the majority declared that another strand of the liberal bundle of rights, disposition at death, could not be abrogated, seemingly because its traditional importance is analogous to the right to exclude others that the Court has already found to be fundamental in *Kaiser Aetna*."
67. Radin, "The Liberal Conception of Property," p. 1676.
68. Radin, "The Liberal Conception of Property," p. 1687.
69. Peterson, Andrea, "The Taking Clause: In Search of Underlying Principles. Part I—A Critique of Current Takings Clause Doctrine," (1989) p. 1362.
70. Peterson, Andrea (1989) p. 1309.
71. Peterson, Andrea (1989) p. 1309.
72. Peterson, Andrea (1989) p. 1312. *See, Board of Regents v. Roth*, 408 U.S. 564 (1972).
73. Peterson, Andrea, "The Takings Clause: In Search of Underlying Principles. Part II—Takings as Intentional Deprivation of Property Without Moral Justification," (1990) p. 59.
74. Peterson, Andrea (1990) p. 90.
75. Peterson, Andrea (1990) p. 91.
76. Peterson, Andrea (1990) p. 106; *see also*, Berger, "A Policy Analysis of The Takings Problem." (1974) p. 174. Berger puts it this way:

> Suffice it to say here that the difficulty with the noxious use doctrine lies in its oversimplified separation of "good" from "bad." Most human activities held to be noxious are, at most, inappropriate to the location or conflict with other uses in the area rather than "bad." The slaughterhouse and the brickyard are socially important and useful, but unfortunately offend our sensibilities when located in residential areas. Nevertheless we all want them to continue somewhere, but elsewhere. A doctrine that allows such activities to be completely destroyed without compensation is without question unfair. (Berger, p. 174).

77. Peterson, Andrea (1990) p. 107. She goes on to say that her principle is able to take account of changes in judgment of wrongdoing over time and geographically. "The moral justification principle takes this factor into account by focusing on whether the lawmakers reasonably believed the conduct at issue would be regarded as blameworthy by the people of that jurisdiction at that time." (p. 110) So, under her principle *Mugler* is not a difficult case to decide. (p. 110)
78. Minda, "The Dilemmas of Property and Sovereignty in the Postmodern Era: New Solutions for the Regulatory Takings

Problem," (1992) p. 134. (Court is moving toward formalism rather than balancing—more *per se* rules.)

For a philosophical treatment of postmodern thought *see*, Rorty, *Philosophy and the Mirror of Nature* (1979).

79. Minda, p. 134.
80. Minda, pp. 155–156n.11.
81. Minda, p. 145. Minda goes on to say: "Rose-Ackerman, however, has so far failed to devise a firm theoretical base in theory to support her eccentric policy approach, nor has she been able to devise a set of formalized rules that enables judges to mediate the conflicting goals of takings law." (p. 146)
82. Minda, p. 158–159n.32.
83. Minda, p. 148.
84. Minda, p.1 48; *See further*, Unger, *The Critical Legal Studies Movement* (1986).
85. The Scalia and Rehnquist approach are reflected in the *Nollan* and *First English* cases of 1987.
86. Michelman, "Takings, 1987," (1988) p. 1601.
87. Michelman, "Takings, 1987," (1988) pp. 1612–1213.
88. Alexander, Gregory S. "Taking, Narrative, and Power," (1988) p. 1772.
89. Fischel, "Introduction," (1988) p. 1584.
90. Karlin, "Back to the Future: From *Nollan* to *Lochner*," (1988) p. 629.
91. Myers, "Some Observations on the Analysis of Regulatory Takings in the Rehnquist Court," (1989) p. 548.
92. Myers (1989) p. 552.
93. Myers (1989) p. 557.
94. Peterson, Craig A., "Land Use Regulatory "Takings" Revisited: The New Supreme Court Approach," (1988) pp. 356–357.
95. Davis & Glicksman, "To the Promised Land: A Century of Wondering and a Final Homeland for Due Process and Takings Clauses," (1989) pp. 437–438.

The *Nollan* case put the Court's stamp of approval on the Unified Model: a police power regulation that lacks proper ends or means constitutes a taking rather than a violation of substantive due process. The case thus moves beyond *Pennsylvania Coal* and creates two categories of regulatory takings: one, based on Relativism, for regulations that "go too far" by imposing excessive economic constraints on the uses of private property; and a second, based on Unification, for regulations lacking a sufficient nexus between their asserted police power ends and the means chosen to accomplish them. In *Nollan*, the Supreme Court held for the first time that land use regulation amounted to a taking of the second kind. It represents the final step in the fusion of the substantive due process and takings limitations on land use regulation referred to by

Justice Stevens in *Moore* and reflected in the two-part takings analysis of
Penn Central and *Agins*. (Davis & Glicksman, pp. 437–438).

96. Davis & Glicksman, p. 442.
97. Davis & Glicksman, p. 401.

CHAPTER SEVEN: THE ECONOMICS OF LAND USE

1. Transaction costs consist of such things as search costs, bargaining
costs, and enforcement costs. That is, costs of finding someone to make
the exchange, costs of finalizing the agreement, and costs of monitoring
and seeing the agreement carried out. For a more elaborate definition of
transaction costs, *see*, Ulen, "The Public Use of Private Property: A
Duel-Constraint Theory of Efficient Governmental Takings," in *Takings
and Just Compensation* (1992) p. 172.
2. Ulen, p. 173.
3. Ulen, p. 174.

> A public good is one that has two closely related characteristics. First, the
> good exhibits nonrivalrous consumption. This means that many people
> may simultaneously consume the good. Examples are firework displays,
> over-the-air (but not cable) radio and television signals, and national
> defense. Second, public goods are those for which private profit
> maximizing suppliers have a difficult time excluding nonpaying
> consumers. (Ulen, p. 174).

4. Tideman, "Takings, Moral Evolution, and Justice," (1988) p. 1723.
5. George, H., *Progress and Poverty* (1880).
6. Fischel, "Introduction," p. 1596.
7. Coase, "The Problem of Social Cost," (1960).
8. Coase, p. 2.
9. Coase, pp. 16–17.

> [W]hen dealing with the problem of the rearrangement of legal rights
> through the market, it was argued that such a rearrangement would be
> made through the market whenever this would lead to an increase in the
> value of production. But this assumed costless market transactions. Once
> the cost of carrying out market transactions are taken into account, it is
> clear that such a rearrangement of rights will only be undertaken when
> the increase in the value of production consequent upon the
> rearrangement is greater than the costs which would be involved in
> bringing it about. When it is less, the granting of an injunction (or the
> knowledge that it would be granted) or the liability to pay damage may
> result in an activity being discontinued (or may prevent its being started)

which would be undertaken if market transactions were costless. (Coase, pp. 16–17).

10. Calabresi & Melamed, "Property Rules, Liability Rules, and Inalienability: One View of the Cathedral," (1972).
11. Berger, "A Policy Analysis" pp. 185–186.

> Professor Calabresi has argued that in the pollution as well as in other areas of liability it is best from an economic efficiency standpoint to assess the costs initially upon the cheapest cost avoider. Calebresi based his analysis upon Coase's notion that, in a system that had no transaction costs, there would be a series of bargains which would culminate in the same allocation of resources—one of economic efficiency—no matter where initial liability lay. But if there are transaction costs, and in the real world there always are, these bargains toward efficiency would not take place where transaction costs exceed the savings made by the move toward efficiency. In that situation it is best to assess the costs upon the cheapest cost avoider as the one who can most easily make the move toward efficiency, thus avoiding higher transaction costs which would otherwise prevent achieving the optimally efficient state. (Berger, pp. 185–186).

12. Calabresi & Melamed, p. 1092.
13. Calabresi & Melamed, p. 1093. "Perhaps the simplest reason for a particular entitlement is to minimize the administrative costs of enforcement." This puts the costs on the party that can avoid them more cheaply. (p. 1096)
14. Calabresi & Melamed, p. 1105.
15. Stigler, "The Theory of Economic Regulation," (1971) p. 5; *see also*, Priest, George L., "The Origins of Utility Regulation and the 'Theories of Regulation' Debate," in *The Journal of Law & Economics* (April 1993).
16. Peltzman, "Toward A More General Theory of Regulation," (1976) p. 212.
17. Peltzman, p. 213.
18. Fischel & Shapiro, "Takings, Insurance, and Michelman: Comments on Economic Interpretations of "Just Compensation" Law," (1988) p. 270.
19. Blume & Rubinfeld, "Compensation for Takings: An Economic Analysis," (1984) p. 571.
20. Blume & Rubinfeld, p. 572.
21. Blume & Rubinfeld, p. 572. "Thus, government-provided insurance represents a potentially attractive alternative. However, for reasons related to private market failure, government-provided insurance must be offered after the fact (*ex post*) in the form of

compensation for regulatory takings, rather than before the fact (*ex ante*)."

22. Blume & Rubinfeld, p. 578. "Yet, Sax fails to analyze all of the efficiency implications of the alternative distributional schemes."

23. Blume & Rubinfeld, pp. 600–601.

24. Blume & Rubinfeld, pp. 618–619.

> "Current" market value as we have defined is an inappropriate measure of compensation. Even if insurance is provided, it ought to be based on the value of the land as it would have been developed had the government not been expected to pay compensation. If current market value is used as a measure of compensation, then any additional investment due solely to the availability of compensation will be included as a part of the compensation payment. This overinvestment due to the presence of compensation is insufficient and should not be encouraged. (Blume & Rubinfeld, pp. 618–619).

25. Epstein, *Takings: Private Property and the Law of Eminent Domain* (1985) pp. 182–183.

26. Epstein (1985) pp. 182–183 (paraphrasing Epstein).

27. Epstein (1985) pp. 182–183.

28. Epstein (1985) p. 183.

29. Epstein (1985) pp. 183–184.

30. Replacement costs are those costs that it would take to replace the original property taken.

31. Epstein (1985) pp. 183–184.

32. Epstein (1985)p. 184 (paraphrasing Epstein).

33. Epstein (1985) p. 185.

34. Epstein (1985) p. 185.

35. 169 U.S. 466 (1898); *see also*, Epstein (1985)(*Smyth v. Ames* is a railroad case. Nebraska established tariffs for the transport of freight and persons. The railroad claimed that it was deprived of a "reasonable return" because of this regulation. Although it was argued under the due process provision, Epstein claims that this was a "vintage" eminent domain case, where property was taken for public use without just compensation. (p. 274, paraphrasing Epstein)).

36. Tarlock, "Regulatory Takings," (1984) p. 33 (citations omitted). *See also*, Costonis, "'Fair' Compensation and the Accommodation Power: Antidotes for the Taking Impasse in Land Use Controversies," (1975).

   See further, Nemmers v. City of Dubuque, 764 F. 2d 502 (8th Cir. 1985) (*Nemmers* was the first effort to attempt to quantify the measure of damages for temporary takings). The *Wheeler* IV test offers a formula for temporary takings. *Wheeler v. City of Pleasant Grove*, 664 F. 2d 99 (5th Cir. 1981), *cert. denied*, 456 U.S. 937 (1982), *appeal after remand, reversed*, 746 F. 2d 1437 (11th Cir. 1984), *appeal after remand*, 833 F. 2d 267 (11th Cir. 1987), *reh'g denied, en banc*, 844 F. 2d 794 (1988), and *appeal after remand*, 896 F. 2d 1347 (1990).

See also, *Herrington v. County of Sonoma*, 834 F. 2d 1488 (9th Cir. 1987), *amended, reh'g denied, en banc*, 857 F. 2d 596 (9th Cir. 1988), *cert. denied*, 489 U.S. 1090 (1989).

See generally, Orgel, *Valuation Under the Law of Eminent Domain* (1953).

37. Michelman (1967) pp. 1214–1215.
38. Ackerman, *Private Property and the Constitution* (1977) pp. 48–49.
39. Ackerman (1977) pp. 48–49; *see also*, Fisher, "The Significance of Public Perceptions of the Takings Doctrine," (1988) p. 1774. (Fisher updates and clarifies Michelman's and Ackerman's utility maximization formula.)
40. Epstein (Book Review), "The Next Generation of Legal Scholarship?" (1978) p. 635 (Reviews Ackerman's book: *Private Property and the Constitution*).
41. Epstein (Book Review) p. 442.
42. Epstein (Book Review) p. 443.
43. Ellickson, "Alternatives to Zoning: Covenants, Nuisance Rules, and Fines as Land Use Controls," (1973) pp. 731–732.
44. Fischel, *The Economics of Zoning Laws* (1985); *see also*, *Regulatory Takings* (1995).
45. Fischel (1985) p. 70.
46. Fischel (1985) p. 70.
47. Fischel (1985) p. 96.
48. Fischel (1985) p. 107.
49. Fischel (1985) pp. 117–118. An externality is a by-product of the production process, whereby its cost is shifted to the community rather than borne or accounted for by the producer or manufacturer.
50. Fischel (1985) pp. 117–118.
51. Fischel (1985) p. 153; *see also*, Coleman, *Markets, Morals and the Law* (1988) pp. 76–81.
52. Fischel (1985) pp. 157–158.
53. Fischel (1985) pp. 158–159.
54. Fischel (1985) pp. 158–159.
55. Fischel (1985) p. 159.

CHAPTER EIGHT: THE POLITICS OF LAND USE

1. What is meant by the term "neighbor" is exactly what the name implies. People, in close proximity to one another, that coalesce around a land use problem in their community, either to maintain a zoning ordinance, change the ordinance, or on a number of other issues. When they bring legal action, the cases they bring are referred to as neighbors cases.
2. Banfield & Wilson, *City Politics* (1966); Elkin, *City and Regime in the American Republic* (1987). (Elkin claims that public officials gain reputation, political visibility, etc., by being associated with large land use projects in their city.) (Elkin, p. 37)
3. Sunstein, *After the Rights Revolution: Reconceiving the Regulatory State* (1990) p. 12. Sunstein argues that regulatory systems are not necessarily inferior to "freedom of contract, private ordering, and largely unfettered markets." He goes on to claim that the modern regulatory state is not unprincipled and has a sense of coherence. Sunstein sees the problem as not one of too much government but of too little government. (paraphrasing Sunstein).
4. Sunstein (1990) p. 19.
5. Sunstein (1990) p. 74.
6. Sunstein, "Paradoxes of the Regulatory State," (1990) pp. 407–441.
7. Sunstein, *After the Rights Revolution,* pp. 2–3.
8. Sunstein, *After the Rights Revolution,* p. 4.
9. Malloy, "A Classical Liberal Critique of Takings Law: A Struggle Between Individualist and Communitarian Norms," (1992) p. 199.
10. Malloy, p. 200.
11. Malloy, p. 204.
12. Malloy, p. 205.

> It is an approach that attempts to strike a balance between the protection of private property rights and the needs of the community in recognition of the fact that although the key referential sign is the individual, individuals do not exit alone and isolated; they exist in community with others. Consequently, a number of wealth transfers can be undertaken by the state even though the taking diminishes the private property of particular individuals for the benefit of others. (Malloy, p. 205).

13. Malloy, p. 207.
14. Wilson, *The Politics of Regulation* (1980) p. 357.

15. Wilson (1980) p. 357; *see also*, Jessop, *State Theory* (1990) chapter 3 (a neo-Marxist attempt to derive a measure of independence of the state from the economic base).
16. Wilson (1980) p. 357.
17. Wilson (1980) p. 359; *see also*, Moe, "Interest, Institutions, and Positive Theory," in *Studies in American Political Development: An Annual* (1987) pp. 236–239, 274–281; *see also*, Stigler, "The Theory of Economic Regulation," (1971).
18. Fischel, *The Economics of Zoning Law*, p. 107.
19. Fischel, *The Economics of Zoning Law*, p. 151. (Quoting J.H. Ely's book *Democracy and Discontent* (1980) pp. 97–98). "First, it is not necessary to elevate property to any special status. Ely argues that the Fifth Amendment's taking clause was not adopted to advance private property beyond the reach of democratic decisions: "On the contrary, the amendment assumes that property will sometimes be taken and provides instead for compensation."" (Fischel, p. 151)
20. Note, "Taking Back Takings: A Coasean Approach to Regulation," (1993), p. 924.
21. Note (1993) p. 924.
22. Friedman, "On Regulation and Legal Process," in *Regulatory Policy and the Social Sciences* (1985) p. 113.
23. Friedman (1985) p. 113.
24. Reich, "The New Property," (1964) p. 733.
25. Reich (1964) p. 772.
26. Reich (1964) p. 772.
27. Reich (1964) p. 773.
28. Martinez, "Reconstructing the Takings Doctrine," (1988) pp. 178–179. ("It is hardly a revelation to positive-law theorists, who assert that property interests exist primarily as they are given legal recognition by the state. It may be a concept with which natural-rights theorists, however, may disagree, because they maintain that property rights exist independently of the state.")

CHAPTER NINE: ABSTRACT PHILOSOPHY OF PROPERTY AND TAKINGS LAW

1. Michelman, "Property, Utility, and Fairness," (1967).
2. Michelman (1967) p. 1204; Locke, *Two Treatises of Government* (1967); Tully, *A Discourse on Property: John Locke and his adversaries* (1980); Carter, *The Philosophical Foundations of Property Rights* (1989).
3. Hegel, *Philosophy of Right*; Michelman (1967) p. 1205.
4. Michelman (1967) pp. 1205–1206n.87.
5. Cohen, "Property and Sovereignty," (1927) p. 18.

6. Cohen (1927) p. 18; *see also*, Munzer, *A Theory of Property* (1990) ("For Hegel "personality" means roughly the self-actualization of the individual through acts of will."(p. 68))

   See also, Ackerman, Bruce A., *Private Property and the Constitution* (1977) p. 184.

   > Put in Hegelian terms, the Ordinary Observer's conception of property is rooted in the egoistic, individualistic consciousness of a member of civil (or market) society who is only marginally concerned with the ethical content of commercial life. In contrast, the Scientific Policymaker's conception is characteristic of Hegel's ideal state official who seeks to reconcile the inevitable conflicts generated by the market society by referring to the community's fundamental ethical principles. (Ackerman, Bruce, p. 184).

7. Epstein, "Possession as the Root of Title," (1979) p. 1224.
8. Epstein, "Possession as the Root of Title," p. 1227.

   > Why does labor itself create any rights in a thing? The labor theory rests upon the belief that each person owns himself (or herself). [Y]et if that possession is good enough to establish ownership of self, then why not possession of external things, unclaimed by others, sufficient as well? [T]he labor theory is called upon to aid the theory that possession is the root of title; yet it depends for its own success upon the proposition that possession of self is the root of title to self. (Epstein, p. 1227).

9. Epstein, "Possession as the Root of Title," p. 1228; *see also*, "On the Optimal Mix of Private and Common Property" in *Social Philosophy & Policy* (Summer, 1994).
10. Tideman, "Takings, Moral Evolution, and Justice," (1988) p. 1724.
11. Tideman (1988) pp. 1725–1726.
12. Tideman (1988) pp. 1728–1729.
13. Honore, "Ownership," (1961) p. 134. Also, Grey is another scholar that has heeded A.M. Honore's analysis that the "thing" should not be left out of the relation. Here is Grey's point: "The substitution of a bundle-of-rights for a thing-ownership conception of property has the ultimate consequences that property ceases to be an important category and political theory."
14. Grunebaum, *Private Property* (1987) p. 3.
15. Grunebaum, (1987) pp. 3–4.
16. Rorty, *Philosophy and the Mirror of Nature* (1979); Derrida, *Of Grammatology* (1976).

BIBLIOGRAPHY

TABLE OF CASES

Agins v. City of Tiburn, 447 U.S. 255 (1980).
Andrus v. Allard, 444 U.S. 51 (1979).
Barron v. Baltimore, 32 U.S. (7 Pet.) 243 (1833).
Bedford v. United States, 192 U.S. 217 (1904).
Berman v. Parker, 348 U.S. 26 (1954).
Brown v. Maryland, 25 U.S. (12 Wheat.) 419 (1827).
Budd v. State of New York, 143 U.S. 517 (1892).
Chicago, Burlington & Quincy R.R. Co. v. Chicago, 166 U.S. 226 (1897).
Chicago, Milwaukee, St. Paul Ry. Co. v. Minnesota, 134 U.S. 418 (1890).
Cincinnati v. Vester, 281 U.S. 439 (1930).
Danforth v. United States, 308 U.S. 271 (1939).
Dolan v. City of Tigard, 114 S. Ct. 2309 (1994).
Eaton v. Boston C. & M. R.R. Co., 51 N.H. 504 (1872).
Euclid v. Ambler Realty Co., 272 U.S. 365 (1926).
First English Evangelical Church v. County of Los Angeles, 482 U.S. 304 (1987).
Florida Rock Industries, Inc. v. United States, 8 Cl. Ct. 160 (1985), *rev.*, 741 F. 2d 893 (Fed. Cir. 1986).
Gibson v. United States, 166 U.S. 269 (1897).
Goldblatt v. Town of Hempstead, 82 S. Ct. 987 (1962).
Griggs v. Alleghny County, 369 U.S. 84 (1962).
Hadacheck v. Sebation, 239 U.S. 394 (1915).
Hanover National Bank v. Moyses, 186 U.S. 181 (1902).
Hawaii Housing Authority v. Midkiff, 467 U.S. 229 (1984).
Herrington v. County of Sonoma, 834 F. 2d 1488 (9th Cir. 1987).
Hodel v. Irving, 107 S. Ct. 2076 (1987).
Hodel v. Virginia Surface Mining & Reclamation Assn. Inc., 452 U.S. 264 (1981).
Home Building & Loan Association v. Blaisdell, 290 U.S. 398 (1934).
Hudson Water Co. v. McCarter, 209 U.S. 349 (1908).
Interstate Railway Co. v. Massachusetts, 207 U.S. 79 (1907).
Just v. Marinette County, 56 Wis. 2d 7 (1972).
Kaiser Aetna v. United States, 444 U.S. 164 (1979).
Keystone Bituminous Coal Association v. DeBenedictis, 480 U.S. 470 (1987).
Kimball Laundry Co. v. United States, 338 U.S. 1 (1949).
Kohl, et al. v. United States, 91 U.S. 367 (1875).
Legal Tender Cases, 12 Wall. 457 (1871).

Leroy Land Development v. Tahoe Regional Planning Agency, 939 F. 2d 696 (9th Cir. 1991).

License Cases, 46 U.S. 504 (1847).

Lochner v. New York, 198 U.S. 45 (1905).

Loretto v. Teleprompter Manhattan CATV Corp., 458 U.S. 419 (1982).

Lucas v. South Carolina Coastal Council, 112 S. Ct. 2886 (1992).

Lynch v. Household Finance Corp., 405 U.S. 538 (1972).

MacDonald, Sommer & Frates v. Yolo County, 477 U.S. 340 (1986).

Miller v. Schoene, 276 U.S. 272 (1928).

Monogahela Navigation Co. v. United States, 148 U.S. 312 (1983).

Moore v. East Cleveland, 431 U.S. 494 (1977).

Mt. Vernon Cotton Co. v. Alabama Power Co., 240 U.S. 30 (1916).

Mugler v. Kansas, 123 U.S. 623 (1887).

Munn v. Illinois, 94 U.S. 113 (1877).

Nectow v. Cambridge, 277 U.S. 183 (1928).

Nemmers v. City of Dubuque, 764 F. 2d 502 (8th Cir. 1985).

Nollan v. California Coastal Commission, 483 U.S. 825 (1987).

Omnia Commercial Co. v. United States, 261 U.S. 502 (1923).

Peabody v. United States, 231 U.S. 530 (1913).

Penn Central Transp. Co. v. City of New York, 483 U.S. 104 (1978).

Pennell v. City of San Jose, 108 S. Ct. 849 (1988).

Pennsylvania Coal Co. v. Pennsylvania, 260 U.S. 393 (1922).

Plymouth Coal Co. v. Pennsylvania, 232 U.S. 531 (1914).

Poletown Neighborhood Council v. City of Detroit, 410 Mich. 616 (1981).

Portsmouth Harbor Land & Hotel Co. v. United States, 250 U.S. 1 (1919).

Preseault v. I.C.C., 110 S. Ct. 914 (1990).

Prune Yard Shopping Center v. Robins, 447 U.S. 74 (1980).

Pumpelly v. Green Bay Co., 80 U.S. (13 Wall.) 166 (1871).

Radiooptics, Inc. v. United States, 621 F. 2d 1113 (1980).

Richmond, Fredricksburg & Potomac Ry. Co., 96 U.S. 521 (1877).

Ridge Co. v. Los Angeles, 262 U.S. 700 (1923).

Bridge Co. v. United States, 105 U.S. 70 (1881).

Ruckelshaus v. Monsanto Co., 467 U.S. 986 (1984).

San Diego Gas & Electric Co. v. City of San Diego, 450 U.S. 621 (1981).

Slaughter-House Cases, 83 U.S. (16 Wall.) 36 (1873).

Smyth v. Ames, 169 U.S. 466 (1898).

Sweet v. Rechel, 159 U.S. 380 (1895).

Transportation Co. v. Chicago, 99 U.S. 635 (1878).

United States v. Carolene Products Co., 304 U.S. 144 (1938).

United States v. Causby, 328 U.S. 256 (1946).

United States v. Commodities Trading Corp., 339 U.S. 121 (1950).

ARTICLES

Alexander, Gregory S. "Taking, Narrative, and Power." 88 *Columbia Law Review* 1752 (1988).

Alexander, Larry. "Takings of Property and Constitutional Serendipity." 41 *University of Miami Law Review* 223 (1986).

Bauman, Gus. "*Hamilton Bank*: No Decision on the Compensation Issue." In *1986 Zoning and Planning Handbook*. Edited by J. Benjamin Gailey. New York: Clark Boardman Co., 1986.

Been, Vicki. ""Exit" as a Constraint on Land Use Exactions: Rethinking the Unconstitutional Conditions Doctrine." 91 *Columbia Law Review* 473 (1991).

Bender, Leslie. "The Takings Clause: Principle or Politics?" 34 *Buffalo Law Review* 735 (1985).

Berger, Lawrence. "A Policy Analysis of the Taking Problem." 49 *New York University Law Review* 165 (1974).

Berger, Michael M. "*Lucas v. South Carolina Coastal Council*: Yes, Virginia, There Can Be Partial Takings." In *Takings: Land-Development Conditions and Regulatory Takings after Dolan and Lucas*. Chicago: American Bar Association Section of State and Local Government Law, 1996.

Berger, Michael M. & Gideon Kanner. "Thoughts on the *White River Junction Manifesto:* A Reply to the "Gang of Five's" Views on Just Compensation for Regulatory Takings of Property." 19 *Loyola (LA) Law Review* 685 (1986).

Bley, Kenneth B. "Substantive Due Process and Land Use: The Alternative to a Takings Claim." In *Takings: Land-Development Conditions and Regulatory Takings after Dolan and Lucas*. Chicago: American Bar Association Section of State and Local Government Law, 1996.

Blume, Lawrence & Daniel L. Rubinfeld. "Compensation for Takings: An Economic Analysis." 72 *California Law Review* 569 (1984).

Bosselman, Fred P. "Land As a Privileged Form of Property." In *Takings: Land-Development Conditions and Regulatory Takings after Dolan and Lucas*. Edited by David L. Callies. Chicago: American Bar Association Section of State and Local Government Law, 1996.

Burton, Bruce W. "Regulatory Takings and the Shape of Things to Come: Harbingers of a Takings Clause Reconstellation." 72 *Oregon Law Review* 603 (1993).

Calabresi, Guido & A. Douglas Melamed. "Property Rules, Liability Rules, and Inalienability: One View of the Cathedral." 85 *Harvard Law Review* 1089 (1972).

Callies, David L. "After *Lucas* and *Dolan*: An Introductory Essay." In *Takings: Land-Development Conditions and Regulatory Takings after Dolan and Lucas.* Edited by David L. Callies. Chicago: American Bar Association Section of State and Local Government Law, 1996.

Carlisle, Richard G. "The Section 1983 Land Use Case: Justice Stevens and the Hunt for the Takings Quark." 16 *Stetson Law Review* 565 (1987).

Coase, R. "The Problem of Social Cost." 3 *Journal of Law & Economics* 1 (1960).

Cohen, Morris R. "Property and Sovereignty." 13 *Cornell Law Review* 8 (1927).

Coletta, Raymond R. "Reciprocity of Advantage and Regulatory Takings: Toward a New Theory of Takings Jurisprudence." 40 *American University Law Review* 297 (1990).

Comment. "The Public Use Limitation on Eminent Domain: An Advance Requiem." 58 *Yale Law Journal* 599 (1949).

Connors, Catherine. "Back to the Future: The "Nuisance Exception" to the Just Compensation Clause." 19 *Capital University Law Review* 139 (1989).

Converse, R.G. "Property Rights Legislation: Some Questions." In *Takings: Land-Development Conditions and Regulatory Takings after Dolan and Lucas.* Chicago: American Bar Association Section of State and Local Government Law, 1996.

Costonis, John. "Presumptive and Per Se Takings: A Decisional Model for the Taking Issue." 58 *New York University Law Review* 465 (1983).

———. "'Fair' Compensation and the Accommodation Power: Antidotes for the Taking Impasse in Land Use Controversies." 75 *Columbia Law Review* 1021 (1975).

Curtin, Jr., Daniel J. "Takings in the Land-Use Arena after *Lucas* and *Dolan*: How Far Is Too Far in Imposing Exactions?" In *Takings: Land-Development Conditions and Regulatory Takings after Dolan and Lucas.* Chicago: American Bar Association Section of State and Local Government Law, 1996.

Davis, Michael J. & Robert L. Glicksman. "To the Promised Land: A Century of Wandering and a Final Homeland for the Due Process and Takings Clauses." 68 *Oregon Law Review* 393 (1989).

Demsetz, Harold. "Toward a Theory of Property Rights." *American Economic Review.* Vol. LVII no. 2 (1967).

Dunham, Allison. "*Griggs v. Alleghany County* in Perspective: Thirty Years of Supreme Court Expropriation Law." 1962 *Supreme Court Review* 63 (1962).

Ellickson, Robert C. "Alternatives to Zoning: Covenants, Nuisance Rules, and Fines as Land Use Controls." 40 *University of Chicago Law Review* 681 (1973).

Epstein, Richard A. "On the Optimal Mix of Private and Common Property." In *Social Philosophy & Policy*, Vol.11 no.2 (Summer 1994).

―――. "Takings: Of Maginot Lines and Constitutional Compromises." In *Liberty, Property, and the Future of Constitutional Development*. Edited by Ellen Frankel Paul & Howard Dickman. New York: State University of New York Press, 1990.

―――. "An Outline on *Takings*." 41 *University of Miami Law Review* 3 (1986).

―――. "Possession as the Root of Title," 13 *Georgia Law Review* 1221 (1979).

―――. Book Review. "The Next Generation of Legal Scholarship?" 30 *Stanford Law Review* 635 (1978).

―――. "A Last Word on Eminent Domain." 41 *University of Miami Law Review* 253 (1973).

Fawcett, David B. "Eminent Domain, The Police Power, and the Fifth Amendment: Defining the Domain of the Takings Analysis." 47 *University of Pittsburgh Law Review* 491 (1986).

Fischel, William A. "Introduction: Utilitarian Balancing and Formalism in Takings." 88 *Columbia Law Review* 1581 (1988).

Fischel, William A. & Perry Shapiro. "Takings, Insurance, and Michelman: Comments on Economic Interpretation of "Just Compensation" Law." 17 *Journal of Legal Studies* 269 (1988).

Fisher, William W. "The Significance of Public Perception of the Takings Doctrine." 88 *Columbia Law Review* 1774 (1988).

Frankfurter, Felix & Henry M. Hart, Jr. "Rate Regulation," In *The Crises of the Regulatory Commission*. Edited by Paul MacAvoy. New York: W.W.Norton & Co., 1970.

Freilich, Robert H. "Public Improvements and the Nexus Requirements: The Takings Equation after *Dolan v. City of Tigard*." In *Institute on Planning, Zoning, and Eminent Domain*. Edited by Carol J. Holgren. New York: Matthew Bender, 1995.

Freilich, Robert H., Elizabeth A. Gavin, & Duane A. Martin. "Regulatory Takings: Factoring Partial Deprivations into the Taking Equation." *In Takings: Land-Development Conditions and Regulatory Takings after Dolan and Lucas*. Chicago: American Bar Association Section of State and Local Government Law, 1996.

Friedman, Lawrence. "On Regulation and Legal Process." In *Regulatory Policy and the Social Sciences*. Edited by Roger G. Noll. University of California Press, 1985.

Gaus, Gerald F. "Property, Rights, and Freedom." In *Social Philosophy & Policy*. Vol. 11 no. 2 (Summer 1994).

Grey, Thomas C. "The Malthusian Constitution." 41 *University of Miami Law Review* 21 (1986).

———. "The Disintegration of Property." In *Property*. Edited by J. Rolond Pennock & J.W. Chapman. NOMOS monograph no. 22. New York: New York University Press, 1980.

Halper, Louise A. "Why the Nuisance Knot Can't Undo the Takings Muddle." In *1996 Zoning and Planning Law Handbook*. Edited by Alan M. Forrest. New York: Clark, Boardman & Callaghan, 1996.

———. "Christopher G. Tiedman, 'Laissez-Faire Constitutionalism' and the Dilemmas of Small-Scale Property in the Gilded Age." 51 *Ohio St. Law Journal* 1349 (1990).

Hill, G. Richard, "Partial Takings after *Dolan*." In *Takings: Land-Development Conditions and Regulatory Takings after Dolan and Lucas*. Chicago: American Bar Association Section of State and Local Government Law, 1996.

Hoff, Arthur Len. "Development of the Concept of Eminent Domain." 42 *Columbia Law Review* 596 (1942).

Honore, A.M. "Ownership." In *Oxford Essays in Jurisprudence*. Edited by A.G. Guest. Oxford: Clarendon Press, 1961.

Karlin, Norman. "Back To The Future: From *Nollan* to *Lochner*." 17 *Southwestern University Law Review* 627 (1988).

Kendall, Douglas T. & James E. Ryan, ""Paying" for the Change: Using Exactions and Sidestep *Nollan* and *Dolan*." In *1996 Zoning and Planning Law Handbook*. Edited by Alan M. Forrest. New York: Clark, Boardman & Callaghan, 1996.

Kmiec, Douglas W. "At Last, the Supreme Court Solves the Takings Puzzle." In *Takings: Land-Development Conditions and Regulatory Takings after Dolan and Lucas*. Chicago: American Bar Association Section of State and Local Government Law, 1996.

Large, Donald W. "The Supreme Court and the Takings Clause: The Search for a Better Rule." 18 *Environmental Law* 3 (1987).

Lawrence, Nathaniel S. "Regulatory Takings: Beyond the Balancing Test." 20 *Urban Lawyer* 389 (1988).

Lipsker, Ross B. & Rebeca L. Heldt. "Regulatory Takings: A Contract." 16 *Fordham Urban Law Journal* 195 (1988).

Macey, Jonathan R. "Property Rights, Innovation, and Constitutional Structure." In *Social Philosophy & Policy*. Vol. 11 no.2 (Summer 1994).

Malloy, Robin P. "A Classical Liberal Critique of Takings Law: A Struggle Between Individualist and Communitarian Norms." In

Taking Property and Just Compensation: Law and Economics Perspectives of the Takings Issue. Edited Nicholas Mercuro Boston: Kluwer Academic Publishers, 1992.

Mandelker, Daniel R. "Investment-Backed Expectations in Takings Law." In *Takings: Land-Development Conditions and Regulatory Takings after Dolan and Lucas.* Chicago: American Bar Association Section of State and Local Government Law, 1996.

―――. "Waiving the Taking Clause: Conflicting Signals from the Supreme Court." In *Institute on Planning, Zoning, and Eminent Domain.* Edited by Carol J. Holgren. New York: Matthew Bender, 1995.

―――. "Of Mice and Missiles: A True Account of *Lucas v. South Carolina Coastal Council.*" In *1994 Zoning and Planning Law Handbook.* Edited by Kenneth H. Young. New York: Clark, Boardman, & Callaghan, 1994.

―――. "The Taking Issue in Land Use Regulation." In *The Land Use Policy Debate in the United States.* Edited by Judith I. de Neufville. New York & London: Plenum Press, 1981.

Martinez, John. "Reconstructing The Takings Doctrine." 16 *Fordham Urban Law Journal* 157 (1988).

McGinley, P. "Regulatory "Takings": The Remarkable Resurrection of Economic Substantive Due Process." In *1988 Zoning and Planning Law Handbook.* Edited by Noah J. Gordon. New York: Clark Broadman Co., 1988.

Michelman, Frank I. "Tutelary Jurisprudence and Constitutional Property." In *Liberty, Property, and the Future of Constitutional Development.* Edited by Ellen Frankel Paul & Howard Dickman. New York: State University of New York Press, 1990.

―――. "Takings, 1987." 88 *Columbia Law Review* 1600 (1988).

―――. "Localism and Political Freedom." In *The Land Use Policy Debate in the United States.* Edited by Judith I. de Neufville. New York & London: Plenum Press, 1981).

―――. "Property, Utility, and Fairness: Comments on the Ethical Foundation of "Just Compensation" Law." 80 *Harvard Law Review* 1165 (1967).

Minda, Gary. "The Dilemmas of Property and Sovereignty in the Postmodern Era: New Solutions for the Regulatory Takings Problem." In *Taking Property and Just Compensation: Law and Economics Perspectives of the Takings Issue.* Edited by Nicholas Mercuro. Boston: Kluwer Academic Publishers, 1992.

Moe, Terry M. "Interests, Institutions, and Positive Theory: The Politics of the NLRB." In *Studies in American Political Development: An Annual.* Edited by Karen Orren & Stephen Skowronek. Vol. 2. New Haven & London: Yale University Press, 1987.

Munzer, Stephen R. "Compensation and Government Takings of Private Property." In *Compensatory Justice*. Nomos XXXIII. New York & London: New York University Press, 1991.

Myers, David. "Some Observations on the Analysis of Regulatory Takings in the Rehnquist Court." 23 *Valparaiso University Law Review* 527 (1989).

Nedelsky, Jennifer. "American Constitutionalism and the Paradox of Private Property." In *Constitutionalism and Democracy*. Edited by Jon Elster & Rune Slagstad. Cambridge: Cambridge University Press, 1988.

Note. "Taking Back Takings: A Coasean Approach To Regulation." 106 *Harvard Law Review* 914 (1993).

Orren, Karen. "Labor Regulation and Constitutional Theory in the United States and England." 22 *Political Theory* 98 (1994).

Paul, Ellen Frankel. "Public Use: A Vanishing Limitation on Government Takings." In *Economic Liberties and the Judiciary*, Edited by James A Dorn & Henry G. Manne. Fairfax, Virginia: George Mason University Press, 1987.

————. "A Reflection on Epstein and His Critics." 41 *University of Miami Law Review* 235 (1986).

————. "Taking by Regulation: Resolving the Constitutional Muddle." In *Constitutional Economics*. Edited by Richard B. McKenzie. D.C. Heath & Co. Lexington MA & Toronto: Lexington Books, 1984.

Peltzman, Sam. "Toward a More General Theory of Regulation." 19 *Journal of Law and Economics* 211 (1976).

Peterson, Andrea. "The Taking Clause: In Search of Underlying Principles. Part I—A Critique of Current Takings Clause Doctrine." 77 *California Law Review* 1299 (1989).

————. "The Taking Clause: In Search of Underlying Principles. Part II—Taking as Intentional Deprivation of Property Without Moral Justification." 78 *California Law Review* 55 (1990).

Peterson, Craig A. "Land Use Regulatory "Takings" Revisited: The New Supreme Court Approaches." 39 *Hastings Law Journal* 335 (1988).

Priest, George L. "The Origins of Utility and the "Theories of Regulation" Debate." In *The Journal of Law & Economics*. Vol. XXXVI (1)(pt. 2) (April 1993).

Radin, Margaret Jane. "Diagnosing the Takings Problem," In *Compensatory Justice*. Edited by John W. Chapman, Nomos XXXIII. New York & London: New York University Press, 1991.

————. "The Liberal Conception of Property: Cross Currents in the Jurisprudence of Takings." 88 *Columbia Law Review* 1667 (1988).

————. "The Consequences of Conceptualism." 41 *University of Miami Law Review* 239 (1986).

————. "Property and Personhood." 34 *Stanford Law Review* 957 (1982).

Rawls, John. "Justice as Fairness." 67 *Philosophical Review* 164 (1958).

Reich, Charles A. "The New Property." 73 *Yale Law Journal* 733 (1964).

Reznick, Scott M. (Comment). "Land Use Regulation and the Concept of Takings in Nineteenth Century America," 40 *University of Chicago Law Review* 854 (1973).

Rose, Carol M. "Property as Wealth, Property as Propriety." In *Compensatory Justice.* Nomos XXXIII. Edited by John W. Chapman. New York & London: New York University Press, 1991.

Rose, Carol M. "*Mahon* Reconsidered: Why the Takings Issue Is Still a Muddle." 57 *Southern California Law Review* 561 (1984).

Rose-Ackerman, Susan. "Against Ad Hockery: A Comment on Michelman." 88 *Columbia Law Review* 1697 (1988).

Ross, Thomas. "Modeling and Formalism in Takings Jurisprudence." 61 *Notre Dame Law Review* 372 (1986).

Sachman, Julius L. "The Right to Condemn." 29 *Albany Law Review* 177 (1965).

Sax, Joseph L. "Takings, Private Property and Public Rights." 81 *Yale Law Journal* 149 (1971).

————. "Takings and The Police Power." 74 *Yale Law Journal* 36 (1964).

————. Book Review. "Takings." 53 *University of Chicago Law Review* 279 (1986).

Smith, James Charles. (Book Review). "The Transformation of American Law." 1977 *Wisconsin Law Review* 1253 (1977).

Sterk, Stewart E. "*Nollan,* Henry George, and Exactions." 88 *Columbia Law Review* 1731 (1988).

Stigler, George. "The Theory of Economic Regulation." 2 *Bell Journal of Economics* 3 (1971).

St. Jeanos, Christopher J. "*Dolan v. Tigard* and the Rough Proportionality Test: Roughly Speaking, Why Isn't Nexus Enough?" In *1996 Zoning and Planning Handbook.* Edited by Alan M. Forrest. New York: Clark, Boardman & Callaghan, 1996.

Sugameli, Glenn P. "Takings Issues in Light of *Lucas v. South Carolina Coastal Council*: A Decision Full of Sound and Fury Signifying

Nothing." In *1994 Zoning and Planning Law*. Edited by Kenneth H. Young. New York: Clark, Boardman & Callaghan, 1994.

Sunstein, Cass R. "Paradoxes of the Regulatory State." 57 *University of Chicago Law Review* 407 (1990).

———. "Naked Preferences and the Constitution." 84 *Columbia Law Review* 1689 (1984).

Tideman, T. Nicholaus. "Takings, Moral Evolution, and Justice." 88 *Columbia Law Review* 1714 (1988).

Treanor, William M. (Comment) "The Origins and Original Significance of the Just Compensation Clause of the Fifth Amendment." 94 *Yale Law Journal* 694 (1985).

———. "The Original Understanding of the Takings Clause and the Political Process." In *1996 Zoning and Planning Law Handbook*. Edited by Alan M. Forrest. New York: Clark, Boardman & Callaghan, 1996.

Ulen, Thomas S. "The Public Use of Private Property: A Duel-Constraint Theory of Efficient Governmental Taking." In *Taking Property and Just Compensation: Law and Economics Perspectives of the Takings Issue*. Edited by Nicholas Mercuro (Boston: Kluwer Academic Publishers, 1992.

Waldron, Jeremy. "The Advantages and Difficulties of the Humean Theory of Property." In *Social Philosophy & Policy*. Vol. 11 no.2 (Summer 1994).

Williams, Jr., Norman. "A Narrow Escape." In *1994 Zoning and Planning Law Handbook*. Edited by Kenneth H. Young. New York: Clark, Boardman & Callaghan, 1994.

Williams, Jr., Norman R. & Holly Ernst. "And Now We Are Here On A Darkling Plain." 13 *Vermont Law Review* 635 (1989).

Williams, Jr., Norman R. Marlin Smith, et al. "The White River Junction Manifesto." 9 *Vermont Law Review* 193 (1984).

Wiseman, Patrick. "When The End Justifies The Means: Understanding Takings Jurisprudence in a Legal System With Integrity." 63 *St. John's Law Review* 433 (1988).

BOOKS

Ackerman, Bruce A. *Private Property and The Constitution*. New Haven & London: Yale University Press, 1977.

Anderson, Robert M. *American Law of Zoning 3d*. New York: The Lawyers Co-Operative Publishing Co., 1986.

Andrews, Richard N.L. *Land in America: Commodity or Resource?* Lexington, MA & Toronto: Lexington Books, 1979.

Banfield, Edward C. & James Q. Wilson. *City Politics*. New York: Vintage Books, 1966.

Bosselman, F., D. Callies, & J. Banta. *The Taking Issue*. Washington, D.C.: Council on Environmental Quality, 1973.

Carr, R.K. *The Supreme Court and Judicial Review*. New York: Rinehart & Co., 1942.

Carter, Alan. *The Philosophical Foundations of Property Rights*. New York: Harvester Wheatsheaf, 1989.

Coleman, Jules L. *Markets, Morals and the Law*. Cambridge: Cambridge University Press, 1988.

Coyle, Dennis J. *Property and the Constitution: Shaping Society Through Land Use Regulation*. New York: State University of New York Press, 1993.

Derrida, Jacques. *Of Grammatology*. trans. by Gayatri Chakravorty Spivak. Baltimore: Johns Hopkins University Press, 1976.

Elkin, Stephen L. *City and Regime in the American Republic*. Chicago: The University of Chicago Press, 1987.

Ely, James W. *The Guardian of Every Other Right: A Constitutional History of Property Rights*. New York & Oxford: Oxford University Press, 1992.

Ely, John Hart. *Democracy and Distrust: A Theory of Judicial Review*. Cambridge, MA: Harvard University Press, 1980.

Epstein, Richard A. *Takings: Private Property and the Law of Eminent Domain*. Cambridge, MA: Harvard University Press, 1985.

—————. *Bargaining with the State*. Princeton, N.J.: Princeton University Press, 1993.

Fischel, William A. *The Economics of Zoning Laws: A Property Rights Approach to American Land Use Controls. paperback edition*. Baltimore & London: The Johns Hopkins University Press, 1987.

—————. *Regulatory Takings: Law, Economics, and Politics*. Cambridge, MA: Harvard University Press, 1995.

Freund, Ernest. *The Police Power, Public Policy and Constitutional Rights*. Chicago: Callaghan & Co., 1904.

Friedman, Lawrence M. *American Law*. New York: W.W. Norton & Co., 1984.

George, Henry. *Progress and Poverty*. New York: Appleton, 1880.

Gifis, Steven H. *Law Dictionary*. Woodbury, NY: Barron's Educational Series, Inc., 1984.

Gillman, Howard. *The Constitution Besieged: The Rise and Demise of Lochner Era Police Power Jurisprudence*. Durham & London: Duke University Press, 1993.

Goldstein, Leslie Friedman. *In Defense of the Text: Democracy and Constitutional Theory*. Maryland: Rowman & Littlefield Publishers, Inc., 1991.

Grunebaum, James O. *Private Ownership*. London & New York: Routledge & Kegan Paul, 1987.

Hartz, Louis. *The Liberal Tradition in America: An Interpretation of American Political Thought Since the Revolution*. New York: Harcourt, Brace, 1955.

Heap, Shaun Hargreaves. *Rationality in Economics*. New York: Basil Blackwell, 1989.

Hegel, G.W.F. *The Philosophy of Right*. trans. by T.M. Knox. Oxford: Oxford University Press, 1942.

Horwitz, M. *The Transformation of American Law*, 1780–1860. Cambridge, MA: Harvard University Press, 1977.

Jessop, Bob. *State Theory: Putting Capitalist States in their Place*. University Park, PA: The Pennsylvania State University Press, 1990.

Kant, Immanuel. *Critique of Pure Reason*. Trans. by Norman Kemp Smith. New York: St. Martin's Press, 1965.

Linowers, R. Robert & Don T. Allensworth. *The Politics of Land-Use Law: Developers vs. Citizens Groups in Courts*. New York: Praeger Publishers, 1976.

Locke, John. *Two Treatises of Government*. Edited by Peter Laslett, 2nd ed. Cambridge: Cambridge University Press, 1967.

Mercuro, Nicholas & Timothy P. Ryan. *Law, Economics and Public Policy*. Greenwich, CT: JAI Press, Inc., 1984.

Munzer, Stephen R. *A Theory of Property*. Cambridge: Cambridge University Press, 1990.

Nozick, Robert. *Anarchy, State, and Utopia*. New York: Basic Books, Inc., 1974.

O'Looney, John. *Economic Development and Environmental Control: Balancing Business and Community in an Age of NIMBYs and LULUs*. CT & Oxford: Quorum Books, 1995.

Orgel, Lewis. *Valuation Under The Law of Eminent Domain*. 2nd ed. Charlottesville, VA: The Michie Co., 1953.

Paul, A.M. *Conservative Crises and the Rule of Law: Attitudes of Bar and Bench 1887–1895*. New York: Cornell University Press, 1960.

Pigou, A.C. *The Economics of Welfare*. 4th ed. London: Macmillan & Co., 1932.

Platt, Rutherford H. *Land Use Control: Geography, Law, and Public Policy* . New Jersey: Prentice Hall, 1991.

Pocock, J.G.A. *The Machiavellian Moment: Florentine Political Thought and the Atlantic Republican Tradition*. Princeton, N.J.: Princeton University Press, 1975.

Popper, Frank J. *The Politics of Land-Use Reform*. Wisconsin: The University of Wisconsin Press, 1981.

Rawls, John. *A Theory of Justice*. Cambridge, MA: Harvard University Press, 1971.

Rose-Ackerman, Susan. *Rethinking the Progressive Agenda: The Reform of the American Regulatory State*. New York: Free Press, 1992.

Rorty, Richard. *Philosophy and the Mirror of Nature*. Princeton, NJ: Princeton University Press, 1979.

Ryan, Alan. *Property*. Minneapolis: University of Minnesota Press, 1987.

Sackman, Julius L. & Patrick J. Rohan. eds. *Nichol's The Law of Eminent Domain*, revised 3rd ed. Mathew Bender, 1994.

Schlatter, Richard. *Private Property: History of an Idea*. New York: Russell & Russell, 1973.

Schultz, David A. *Property, Power, and American Democracy*. New Brunswick, NJ: Transaction Publishers, 1992.

Sunstein, Cass R. *After the Rights Revolution: Reconceiving the Regulatory State*. Cambridge, MA: Harvard University Press, 1990.

Tiedeman, Christopher G. *A Treatise on The Limitations of Police Power in the United States*. St. Louis: The F.H. Thomas Law Book Co., 1886.

Tully, James. *A Discourse on Property: John Locke and his adversaries*. Cambridge: Cambridge University Press, 1980.

Unger, Roberto Mangabeira. *The Critical Legal Studies Movement*. Cambridge, MA: Harvard University Press, 1986.

Williams, Norman & John M. Taylor. eds. *Williams American Planning Law: Land Use and the Police Power*. Callaghan, 1988 revision.

Wilson, James Q. ed. *The Politics of Regulation*. New York: Basic Books, 1980.

Wood, Gordon. *The Creation of the American Republic*, 1776–1787. Chapel Hill, N.C.: University of North Carolina, 1969.

INDEX

ABOUT THE AUTHOR

 **George Skouras** is a New York attorney currently completing his Ph.D. in Political Science at The New School for Social Research, Graduate Faculty of Political and Social Science. He has also published legal material regarding punitive damages in the transport and handling of hazardous and toxic substances.

STUDIES IN LAW AND POLITICS

The new series Studies in Law and Politics is devoted to texts and monographs that explore the multidimensional and multi-disciplinary areas of law and politics. Subject matters to be addressed in this series include, but will not be limited to: constitutional law; civil rights and liberties issues; law, race, gender, and gender orientation studies; law and ethics; women and the law; judicial behavior and decision-making; legal theory; sociology of law; comparative legal systems; criminal justice; courts and the political process; and other topics on the law and the political process that would be of interest to law and politics scholars. Submission of single-author and collaborative studies, as well as collections of essays are invited.

The series editor is: Dr. David Schultz
1120 St. Clair Avenue
St. Paul, MN 55105